"This book is an important and timely contribution to theological discourse. For more than two decades, I have known Khristi as a leader, mentor, and author who has played a significant role in shaping the emerging theology of numerous Black girls. *Womanish Theology* offers fresh ethnographic perspectives and gives voice to these girls, who have a lot to teach us about the nature, significance, and agency of God in our modern world."

—**Cleve V. Tinsley IV**, assistant professor of history and political science, executive director, Center for African American History and Culture, Virginia Union University

"One thing is for sure: Khristi Adams is not and never will be a game! In *Womanish Theology* she describes a faith path for Black girls and women in a way that feels both hero and homegirl. This is required reading for all of us!"

—**Candice Marie Benbow**, author of *Red Lip Theology*

"Khristi Adams is a consistent and credible voice for young Black women. In *Womanish Theology*, she generously takes us on a journey of the spiritual dimensions of her Black girlhood while unpacking the complex, developing, and rich theological wanderings of the contemporary Black girls and young women featured in this one-of-a-kind work. I found myself reclaiming and cherishing anew my own Black girl spiritual development journey."

—**Christina H. Edmondson**, certified cultural intelligence facilitator, public speaker, mental health therapist, and coauthor of *Faithful Antiracism*

"*Womanish Theology* is a bold and brave exploration of the spiritual lives of Black girls and adolescents. Through this collection of instructive testimonies, Khristi Adams offers extraordinary insight into the theological sources that engender hope, faith, and self-love. In taking Black girls' spiritual lives and development seriously, *Womanish Theology* provides an important reminder: children are not just the future of our faith communities, they are also precious interpreters and ambassadors of the faith right now."

—**Jonathan Lee Walton**, president, Princeton Theological Seminary; author of *Watch This! The Ethics and Aesthetics of Black Televangelism* and *A Lens of Love: Reading the Bible in Its World for Our World*

Womanish Theology

Previous Books by Khristi Lauren Adams

Parable of the Brown Girl: The Sacred Lives of Girls of Color

Unbossed: How Black Girls Are Leading the Way

Black Girls Unbossed: Young World Changers Leading the Way

Womanish Theology

Discovering God through the Lens of Black Girlhood

KHRISTI LAUREN ADAMS

BrazosPress
a division of Baker Publishing Group
Grand Rapids, Michigan

Published by Brazos Press
a division of Baker Publishing Group
Grand Rapids, Michigan
BrazosPress.com

Library of Congress Cataloging-in-Publication Data
Names: Adams, Khristi Lauren, author.
Title: Womanish theology : discovering God through the lens of black girlhood / Khristi Lauren Adams.
Description: Grand Rapids, Michigan : Brazos Press, a division of Baker Publishing Group, 2024. | Includes bibliographical references.
Identifiers: LCCN 2024002355 | ISBN 9781587436345 (paperback) | ISBN 9781587436352 (casebound) | ISBN 9781493446414 (ebook)
Subjects: LCSH: African American girls—Religious life. | Girls, Black—Religious life. | Womanism.
Classification: LCC BV4455 .A338 2024 | DDC 248.8/2082—dc23/eng/20240222 LC record available at https://lccn.loc.gov/2024002355

Names and other identifying details of the women interviewed for this book have been changed to protect their identities.

Cover art, Carnaval by Luciano Cian, Bridgeman Images

The author is represented by the literary agency of Embolden Media Group.

24 25 26 27 28 29 30 7 6 5 4 3 2 1

To Mom and Dad,
for teaching me, guiding me,
and showing me the way.
I love you.

CONTENTS

Note from the Author

Sprinkled throughout each chapter of this book you will find quotations from Black women and girls that help capture the diversity and complexity of perspectives in womanish theology. In carrying out my research, I conducted one-on-one and group interviews via Zoom or in person to collect detailed information from each participant. The ages of the participants ranged from ten to seventy years old (with the adult women interviewed reflecting on their girlhood). I used a semistructured interview format to guide each conversation, which allowed those being interviewed to express their thoughts and experiences in their own words. Pseudonyms have been used to protect the privacy of those interviewed.

Acknowledgments

To the Clark and Adams families and to my beloved ancestors, known and unknown: I live my life in honor of each and every one of you.

To the girls of At the Well Leadership Academy, The Hill School, Leadership LINKS, and all the other Black girls and women who took the time to share their experiences and have conversations with me: you are seen, you are valued, you are heard, and you are loved.

Jevon Bolden: I was nervous to get a book agent because I wondered if someone would truly represent me and my ideas with sensitivity and understanding. You have been God's answer to my prayers! Thank you for advocating for me and encouraging me in all my work. I am excited to see how God blesses Embolden Media Group!

Katelyn Beaty: what a joy and a breath of fresh air you have been to work with! Thank you for your friendship and professionalism and for seeing the vision for "womanish theology."

Pastor Soaries: next to my parents, you have been the single greatest influence in my life. I often wonder who I would be had our paths not crossed. There would be no "womanish theology" had there been no Buster Soaries. My faith journey, my advocacy and activism, my theology of justice and passion for community all came from your influence. Thank you for giving me a church to call "home." Thank you for being the best pastor, teacher, and mentor that anyone could ever hope to have.

Mrs. Soaries: you were always more than "first lady" to me. You were the glue that held us all together at the "old" church. You prayed for us always. You cared for us always. Thank you for listening to the Holy Spirit and for helping to guide us accordingly. I appreciate you more than I have expressed.

Ebonee: you have encouraged me from the first time I mentioned this book, all throughout the process of writing it, and celebrated with me when I typed the last few words. You are the friend I don't deserve but the friend I am blessed to have.

And finally, as always, extended family and community of support: I am just an extension of the love with which you have surrounded me. Thank you.

Introduction to Woman*ish* Theology

> . . . as though our lives have no depth and no meaning without the white gaze.
>
> —Toni Morrison, *The Pieces I Am*

At one of my recent book talks, a woman raised her hand and asked, "What would a Black girl theology look like?" I paused to reflect on my first year of seminary, when I had come to initially learn about theology. As a young Black woman in my early twenties, I was lost in the classes because of the depth of theological knowledge my White peers seemed to have come to seminary with. They could quote Karl Barth, the well-known Swiss Protestant theologian. They were familiar with theologians like Reinhold Niebuhr, Friedrich Schleiermacher, and Paul Tillich. We learned not just about those theologians but also about their interpretation of theological and biblical concepts. To me, this was the standard for theological thought: older, White, male theologians. They were the foremost voices of this discipline. I thought White men owned theology.

My early seminary experience was dominated by what Pulitzer Prize–winning novelist Toni Morrison calls the "master narrative" or "the ideological script that is imposed by those who are in authority."[1] White male voices had historically framed and shaped theological study and practice. However, elective classes later introduced me to Black, liberation, mujerista, womanist, and feminist theologies. I came to understand that marginalized voices had always been the centerpiece of Jesus's ministry; therefore, excluding those voices as a significant source of theological knowledge is a mistake.

Theologian Nancy Westfield once wrote, "Too many male scholars have been trained, trained themselves and others, to take private, intimate ideas and experiences of their own lives and convolute them into supposedly universal truths."[2] She references Elizabeth Dodson Gray, who believes that women name the sacred differently than men do. In *Introducing Womanist Theology*, Stephanie Mitchem writes, "Theology begins not in a classroom but in living life. This is a departure from ideas of theology as controlled by the academy. . . . Theology is not the exclusive property of the elite."[3]

To be young, Black, and a girl is to be part of one of the most disenfranchised, socially excluded communities. Why do we exclude Black girlhood from our knowledge of God? Black girlhood is a state of existence and an interdisciplinary field whereby Black girls are recognized as experts of their own experience. Corrine Field and LaKisha Michelle Simmons argue that little attention has been given to Black girlhood and that "distinguishing stages of girlhood—early childhood, adolescence, young womanhood—reveals how each generation first learns about race, gender, and class domination in their families, friend groups, neighborhoods and cities."[4] This, I argue, is also true for how Black girls learn theological concepts at each developmental stage of life. Black girls are a legitimate source of theological knowledge.

When Black women reflect on their lives, many of them tell stories of faith exploration from their childhood. To be sure, many spiritually oriented Black women did not grow up in the church, have had different religious and cultural upbringings, or may not have had any spiritual or religious guidance. We were not all raised in the same way. However, for a specific subset of Black women who grew up with Christian influences, theology began on the margins of Black girlhood. Concepts like prayer, Scripture, justice, suffering, and the image of God were first formed in our minds as girls. Katie Cannon, who has been widely recognized as the founder of the womanist movement, once reflected on thoughts she had as a Black girl at age three. She explains how she went to a Lutheran kindergarten, where she learned the Beatitudes, the Ten Commandments, about sin, and about the love of God. She explains that while being exposed to these teachings, her young mind struggled to understand them alongside the paradox of her own context. She says, "Yet I couldn't understand—and this is a theological question at three years old—what Black people had done where we couldn't go to parks or skating rinks or the library."[5] The beginnings of her womanist frameworks were formed right there at age three.

This book presents a theology from Black girlhood. Womanist theology comes closest to this thought because it is a religious framework that centers the perspectives and experiences of Black women. The womanist tradition naturally assumes Black girlhood and does consider the experiences of Black girls, but I argue that Black girlhood interpretations of theology need their own category. In the preface to her 1983 book, *In Search of Our Mothers' Gardens*, Alice Walker provides a thorough explanation of the origins of the term *womanist*:

> 1. From womanish. (Opp. of "girlish," i.e., frivolous, irresponsible, not serious.) A black feminist of color. From the black folk expression of mothers to female children, "You acting womanish," i.e., like a woman. Usually referring to outrageous, audacious, courageous or willful behavior. Wanting to know more and in greater depth than is considered "good" for one. Interested in grown-up doings. Acting grown up. Being grown up. Interchangeable with another black folk expression: "You trying to be grown." Responsible. In charge. Serious.[6]

Womanist comes from *womanish*. According to Walker, *womanish*, though sometimes seen as derogatory, was how Black mothers described their female children.

Oftentimes, these girls were "interested in grown-up doings." In *What Manner of Woman*, a short documentary film created by the Womanist Institute, the narrator expounds on the unique nature of the term. "Taken from the Black southern expression 'You acting womanish,' mommas, nanas, aunties, church mothers, and other mothers confirmed, critiqued, and challenged their girl children to ensure that they not only survived but thrived in a world often configured to destroy their creativity, intelligence, and womanhood."[7] Renita Weems continues that clarification, saying that "womanist comes from the Black kind of southern folklorish way of talking about 'you are womanish,' meaning that you are fast, it means that you are bold, it means that you break boundaries."[8]

Though *womanish* is more of a behavioral term, I would like to adopt it for the purposes of naming this new theology, particularly since it's at the root of the term *womanist*.

womanist = theology of Black womanhood
womanish = theology of Black girlhood

Womanish theology explores the spirituality of Black girls through various stages of childhood and adolescence. Womanish theology explores grown-up theological concepts through the lens of Black girlhood. The direct perspectives and experiences of Black girls are distinct from womanist theology simply because womanist theology is a methodological approach that centers *adult* Black women. Womanist and womanish theologies are naturally connected, yes, but womanish theology moves away from the adult focus.

When Jesus encourages his disciples to become like children, he challenges us, his followers, to consider young people as teachers and guides who draw us closer to God (see Matt. 18:2–5). Black girls help us construct how we understand theology. In the same way that girlhood studies is distinguished from the field of feminist studies, Black girlhood theology must be distinguished from Black womanhood theology. Black girls deserve their own framework for understanding God, just as adult Black women have their own perspectives. Field and Simmons have similar thoughts about the field of Black girlhood studies needing its own voice: "But what about when Black girls want to define themselves as distinct from Black women? What about the moments when they push back against their elders or celebrate themselves as a new generation in rebellion against the past? Can these moments when Black girls want to be recognized as *not yet* women only undermine Black feminism, or can they strengthen it by deepening appreciation for what women can learn when they listen to girls?"[9]

Furthermore, womanish theology asserts that God doesn't just meet Black women as adults. For many of us, God met us in our girlhood. It was there that our theologies began to form. Black girls can only strengthen the field of theology from this vantage point. Various ideas within womanish theology will, at times, share similarities with other forms of theology. Black girls process salvation, death, service, and other theological concepts just as any other human being. What makes this theology distinct is that these ideas are from their young minds and perspectives. I believe that all Black girls carry within them a theological story.

In reflecting on my own Black girlhood, I realize that the first time I was introduced to theology was not when I entered seminary. Rather, theological concepts had been introduced to me throughout my childhood and adolescence. My friend Jemar Tisby once tweeted, "Different people in different contexts ask different questions and seek different applications of theology. We need each other to do theology well."[10] We certainly need interpretations from Black girlhood to do theology well. This book will seek to answer the question that was asked of me at the book talk I mentioned earlier: What would a Black girl theology look like? I hope an understanding of Black girlhood theology will lead you, dear reader, to a deeper appreciation for yourself and your own spiritual awareness. I hope it challenges you to deconstruct your own ideas of God and self and inspires you to engage with God more authentically outside the "master narrative." Finally, I hope *Womanish Theology* reminds you that Black girls are fellow image bearers, here to point us toward a better understanding of God.

Woman*ish* Theology of Scripture

How Black Girls Interpret the Bible

My first encounters with God were through my foremothers: my great-grandmother Ma Rosella, my grandmother—affectionately known as Mama Hattie—and her identical twin sister, Aunt Mary. In the 1980s they all lived in a one-story, three-bedroom house on Powell Drive in Rocky Mount, North Carolina. My great-uncle Bunk and my aunt Veda lived with them. My aunts, uncle, and mother purchased and took care of the home so that the five of them could live there. My family had a tradition in which the grandchildren spent their summers "down south" in Rocky Mount, where at least seven of us cousins crammed into the tiny space. When I was a child, the space didn't feel so tiny to me. It was like a never-ending maze that could hold the entirety of our collective family.

The house was more than just a house: it was home. That was how we would refer to it when we spoke of visiting. If my mother said, "We'll be heading home for the holidays," she didn't mean our New Jersey house. She meant the house on Powell Drive.

When my family went down south, we always drove. My mom and dad would pack the car with our suitcases, snacks, and sandwiches. My older brother and I would sit in the back seat prepared for the long drive that took only about eight hours but felt like days. When we reached the exit for Rocky Mount, I would feel myself getting more and more excited. Passing the old Belk Department Store, the Piggly Wiggly, and the Gardner's Barbeque Restaurant meant we were getting closer to home. I knew we were just minutes away when we passed Hollomans, because the convenience store was about two blocks from where we would turn onto Powell Drive. As the car pulled up to the house, my brother and I would boil over with excitement. My dad would barely have taken the keys out of the ignition before I opened the car door and ran up to the house and through the front door.

Just inside the house was the main living room, which was spacious and bright. Each area had its own unique smell; the living room smelled of lint balls. A plastic-covered sofa sat against the wall facing the front door. (They had the plastic on the couch to keep the "good" furniture from getting dirty.) A table sat against the front window that we knew to be a special table because on it sat a large, white Bible that was described as "the family Bible." Next to it were pictures of family and a piece of art that had the word *Yahweh* written in Hebrew on it. A portrait of Martin Luther King Jr., another of Black Jesus, and a rendering of the Twenty-Third Psalm hung on the walls of the living room. The living room was not for frivolous play; it was a space to entertain special company. We didn't just hang out in the living room, and if we did, we got in trouble. There was always an abundance of snacks waiting for us in the dining room: pork rinds, Little Debbie Zebra Cakes, Oatmeal Cream Pies, cookies, and candy. The freezer was stocked with ice cream and ice pops that my grandfather, Granddaddy Joe, would bring by. (He lived in another part of Rocky Mount.) Through the dining room was the den, which functioned as an alternate living room, where all of us hung out leisurely. At any given time, twenty of our family and close family friends were in the home at once.

When I entered the house after the long drive down, I would run straight into the kitchen to be greeted by Mama Hattie, who was usually there preparing a meal for us. The kitchen often smelled of pies baking or chicken and dumplings on the stove. If we were visiting around the holidays, stacks of sweet potato pies would be waiting for us on the counter. "Hey, Sugar!" Mama Hattie would say when she saw me, her face glistening with sweat from standing over the hot stove for hours. She would wrap her arms around me, swallow up my small body, and kiss my face a few times. She was home. I was home.

Godly is the word I used to describe my grandmother. She was the first person to introduce me to the faith. I knew her to be the main caretaker for me, my brother, and my cousins when we spent the summer in Rocky Mount. I spent a great deal of time with Mama Hattie, so I got to watch her closely. Like with the home, I can picture her vividly. I can see her sitting in her room on the front corner of her bed leaning toward a side table with a small lamp on it. I can even see what she is wearing. She often wore a thin white robe with small buttons in the front and what looked like splashes of colors, either flowers or butterflies. Most importantly, I can see that she is reading her Bible, held with such love and care. She would often spend the morning sitting on the corner of her bed quietly reading, wearing large, oval reading glasses. We all understood that this was sacred time, and she was not to be disturbed. I would sometimes sit on the opposite side of the bed and watch her. Although she wouldn't acknowledge me until she was finished, she knew I was observing. Sometimes when she wasn't in the room, I would go in and take a sneak peek in her Bible. It was big for my small hands, and the cover was worn. The first page read, "The Holy Bible. Giant Print. King James Version Containing the Old and New Testaments. Red Letter Edition."

On another inside page was "Rosella Rodgers" written in cursive. This Bible had been passed down from her mother, my great-grandmother, Grandma Rosella, who also lived in the home. Within the pages of Scripture were notes in the margins. "By faith and not by sight," one margin read. Scripture passages like "Wait on the LORD" were double underlined, and the word *wait* was circled. I didn't quite understand what any of it meant at the time. I just knew that this was a very important book and that it was from God. Mama Hattie believed in the authority of Scripture. To her, Scripture was like medicine. Scripture had the power to heal. The words were meant to be applied daily to keep us on the right path. I believe this is the reason Mama Hattie, Grandma Rosella, and Aunt Mary were intent on passing down Scripture to all of us. To this day, my mother still owns that Bible.

It was Mama Hattie and not the church that taught me some of the foundational Bible songs. When it was bath time or playtime, she would sing the songs and have me repeat after her. I knew that Mama Hattie believed the lyrics she sang to me, and because of that I trusted the words too. When I reflect on this, I realize those songs were all interpretations of Scripture. I was learning the Bible through the lyrics to the songs. "He's Got the Whole World in His Hands" is a reflection of Psalm 24:1–2: "The earth is the Lord's and the fullness thereof, the world and those who dwell therein, for he has founded it upon the seas and established it upon the rivers" (ESV). "This Little Light of Mine" is about Matthew 5:16: "In the same way, let your light shine before others, so that they may see your good works and give glory to your Father in heaven" (ESV). The song "Jesus Loves Me" is explicit that Jesus loves us. How do we know? "For the Bible tells me so."

Mama Hattie took us to church every Sunday. Sleeping in on Sunday mornings was never an option for anyone in our household or any of our neighbors' households. I wore frilly dresses and patent leather shoes, my brother and male cousins wore suits, and Mama Hattie would have on a dress, with a glorious, wide-brimmed church hat to match. We would all pile into her old wood-paneled station wagon to take the ten-minute drive to Ebenezer Baptist Church. Though I didn't know what a megachurch was at the time, Ebenezer felt like one to me. The large, brown-brick building sat at the end of the first section of Raleigh Road. There was an Ebenezer Baptist Church sign, and the pastor's name, Rev. Thomas L. Walker, was directly underneath. As we walked into the church, we were always greeted by friendly people, all who knew Mama Hattie and the Clark family by name, even if I did not recognize them. In the church lobby, I was always met with cool air and an ambrosial smell that was so distinct that it continues to be difficult to describe and I have only ever associated with Ebenezer. The choir was usually singing or someone would be up front at the altar praying as we entered the sanctuary.

Typically, my brother and cousins would go off to Sunday school, and I would stay with Mama Hattie. As a young girl, I could not comprehend what was happening and would lean over to ask Mama Hattie to explain. One time as the Communion plate was going by and I asked her why I could not take Communion like everyone else, Mama Hattie explained to me that I had to be "saved and baptized" to take Communion. In the Baptist church, unbelievers could not take Communion. I wanted to be baptized, but then I was told that I was too young to understand. I remember hoping that nothing would happen to me before I was old enough to get baptized because I did not want to die as an unbeliever. Yet I was confused because I did believe as I had been taught.

The pastor, Rev. Walker, would walk to the pulpit during the middle of the service. Rev. Walker was a Black man with a very distinctive and commanding presence. He always wore a black and red cape over his suit and shook hands with anyone already behind the pulpit before kneeling to pray at the large chair in the middle and taking his seat. He had a slow, deep, raspy speaking voice that would oftentimes rise as the congregation would yell, "Yes!" and "Amen, Pastor!" throughout the sermon. The message he preached always found its sole source in Scripture. From time to time, Mama Hattie would lean over to see if I was understanding. For the most part, I did not understand, but she would explain as much as she could. At the end of the sermon, Rev. Walker would always sing his signature song, "One Day at a Time."

> One day at a time, sweet Jesus,
> That's all I'm asking of You.[1]

I heard that song so much that one Christmas I asked my parents for the vinyl record that Rev. Walker and his ensemble recorded that included that song. Upon receiving it, I played it repeatedly on my record player over the next few months.

When we stayed in Rocky Mount for the summer, the seven of us cousins would sit around the table for every meal. At the center of the table was a plastic box shaped like a loaf of bread. It was labeled with the words "Our Daily Bread," and in the box were different verses from the King James Version written on small, rectangular cards.

If one of us touched our meal before we read Scripture, we would get in trouble in the form of a slight rap on the hand or a reprimanding glance. Mama Hattie would have us pass around the small box and take out a Scripture passage at random. When we were done, each of us would take a turn reading. This household practice went on every day for breakfast, lunch, and dinner.

"John 6:51," my brother, Shaun, would read. "I am the living bread which came down from heaven: if any man eat of this bread, he shall live for ever: and the bread that I will give is my flesh, which I will give for the life of the world."

My cousin Tara would read, "Psalm 19:14: 'Let the words of my mouth, and the meditation of my heart, be acceptable in thy sight, O Lord, my strength, and my redeemer.'"

Because I was so young and newer to reading, I would read at my own slow pace, "Proverbs 3:5: 'Trust in the Lord with all thine heart; and lean not unto thine own understanding.'"

Reading the Scripture was not enough. Mama Hattie would ask us what it meant to us. I would interpret the Scripture the best I could from my childlike perspective, and even if I was far off topic, Mama Hattie would say there were no wrong answers. She taught us to interpret the words the best we could for ourselves: an integral approach to hermeneutics, which deals with methods of interpreting the Bible. Mama Hattie read the Bible for herself, an approach most commonly known as personal devotion. She, in turn, taught us to read for ourselves as well. My introduction to Scripture was not academic or historical but personal. How else could a six-year-old Black girl find relevance in a centuries-old historical text? I did not understand the nuances of biblical hermeneutics—a term that I would later come to use frequently in seminary. Without knowing it, as a Black woman, Mama Hattie embodied a womanist approach to the Bible.

Mitzi Smith, professor of New Testament at Ashland Theological Seminary, says that within womanist hermeneutics "we privilege our concerns, our voices, our traditions and read biblical text from that standpoint and from that hermeneutical framework."[2] My experience and perspective as a young Black girl would be my lens for interpreting the text. Spiritual Black women have also been known to glean their wisdom from the Bible using their personal relationship with God and their experiences.[3]

Because of our family's history in the Baptist church, Mama Hattie also had a Baptist approach to understanding Scripture. "For Baptists, the Bible is and has always been . . . the final authority in moral responsibility, in theological beliefs, and in human relationships."[4] Through her womanist and Baptist approaches, I aimed to understand Scripture and its importance using my mind as a young Black girl. Some would say their introduction to Scripture was in a church or school setting. Mine was in a small, one-story house in Rocky Mount, North Carolina, in my grandmother's bedroom and at the dining room table. For that I am grateful.

While Mama Hattie spent time teaching us to live life according to the Word, Aunt Mary demonstrated what it meant to walk according to the Word. Growing up, I did not spend as much time with Aunt Mary as I did with Mama Hattie, but I observed her closely. I had more fear of Aunt Mary than Mama Hattie simply because Aunt Mary was no-nonsense. She was a busy woman who worked for the city of Rocky Mount as an administrative aide. She was an active member of Ebenezer Baptist Church and was one of the main Sunday school and Bible study teachers. She prepared food baskets for people in need who lived in the community and often visited those who were sick and shut in. Aunt Mary loved the Lord and was not shy to tell everyone of God's goodness. If you asked Aunt Mary, "How are you doing?" she would respond, "The Lord is with me." If you dared to ask her again, she would respond in a stern tone, "The Lord is with me," as if to say, "I told you the first time." When she said this, she was essentially quoting Psalm 23:1: "The Lord is my shepherd" (KJV), or Matthew 28:20, where Jesus says, "Lo, I am with you always" (KJV). Everyone in the community called her "Aunt Mary." She lived and walked a ministry of care not just for her church but also for our surrounding neighbors. I have often heard stories of how Aunt Mary sat with neighbors at the hospital, brought over meals, or prayed with them in their grief. The Lord was indeed with her.

She was very stern with us grandchildren and was the strictest disciplinarian in the house. One time my brother and cousins and I decided that we wanted to "play church." We assigned different roles to each person: Tara was the preacher, my brother was the organist, "Little Greg" was the drummer, Leah and Rachel were singers in the choir, and Ryan was a greeter. (I don't think they knew what kind of role to assign me, so I was just a member of the congregation.) We orchestrated an entire church service through our childhood perspectives, and when it came time to serve Communion, we found some rolls and made Kool-Aid to distribute. The moment we were getting ready to partake, Aunt Mary arrived home and caught us. By her clenched jaw and furrowed brows, we knew that Aunt Mary was angry. Playing church was sacrilege, and she gave us a verbal lashing that I remember to this day. To Aunt Mary, you did not play with God.

Aunt Mary retired around the time Ma Rosella was diagnosed with cancer. Shortly after that, Mama Hattie was diagnosed with cancer as well. Uncle Bunk, who was also living in the house, had a severe alcohol addiction. The alcoholism eventually caused him to have both an aneurism and a stroke right before my great-grandmother passed. He was left paralyzed on one side of his body, and that in turn affected his speech. Aunt Mary took care of Uncle Bunk, while my grandmother traveled north to live with my aunt, who took care of her. Sadly, Mama Hattie died not long after, and suddenly Aunt Mary was the family matriarch, taking care of Uncle Bunk and Aunt Veda. There was a plethora of justifiable reasons for Aunt Mary to put Uncle Bunk into a care facility. Uncle Bunk could not walk, feed himself, go to the bathroom on his own, or speak clearly. At the time, Aunt Mary was sixty years old. She had her own grief to deal with after losing her mother and twin sister in back-to-back years. An outside person may have thought that a woman caring for this older man on her own was preposterous. But Aunt Mary was adamant about Uncle Bunk not going to a facility. He was her brother. He was family, and in our family, if you have the home and the means, you do not put your family in a facility with strangers to take care of them. We care for our own.

Even though Mama Hattie was gone, we still went down to the family house on Powell Drive each year, sometimes for holidays and sometimes for a little while in the summer. Aunt Mary followed a routine every day. She would wake up and read her Bible and pray, just as Mama Hattie had done. She would check in on Uncle Bunk and then cook his breakfast. Because his stroke left him unable to chew properly, she would chop up his food like baby food. She did not have a food processor, so she would grind the food by hand. After putting his food on the tray, she would go into his room, and he would not eat until they prayed. Anyone in the house could hear this prayer because it was loud and resounding. "Our Father!" Aunt Mary would scream. Uncle Bunk would repeat after her in a garbled tone, "Our Father." She would then say, "Who art in heaven!" "Who art in heaven," he would repeat. They would continue that way until the end of the Lord's Prayer, and then she would feed him his food. As a child, I would sometimes go in during the prayer or to say hi to Uncle Bunk. He would always greet me, although I could never make out what he was saying. The TV was usually on a program like *Sanford and Son*, *What's Happening!!*, or *The Jeffersons*. At times he would try to feed himself, and Aunt Mary was always patient with him. He would slowly put food into his mouth, and sometimes the food would drop onto the napkin that was tucked into his shirt.

Though Aunt Mary was his main caregiver, Uncle Bunk had in-home care during the daytime. Our family made sure that he had some of the best home health aides. At times the home aides would bathe Uncle Bunk, get him dressed, put him into his wheelchair, and wheel him out to the living room to sit. I suppose it was a change of scenery for Uncle Bunk. When we were home, there was a lot of activity in the house, and sitting in the living room, Uncle Bunk could be a part of that family time. The home aides also gave Aunt Mary a break. She would get up early in the morning and go to yard sales, the grocery store, or church. When she could not go to church, church members would bring her tapes of the sermons. Rev. Walker also made sure to stop by the house to visit and pray with Aunt Mary. Sometimes he would come to see the whole family when we were in town.

Still, Aunt Mary's entire life was taking care of her brother, which she did from 1988 to 2012, when he died. She took care of Uncle Bunk for twenty-four years. As a child, I thought what she did for Uncle Bunk was normal. It wasn't until I was older that I realized just how extraordinary her act of care was. Her unconditional love, expressed in patient action, was, in fact, abnormal. To observe Aunt Mary was to observe Jesus. During his ministry, Jesus had profound care for the sick and the suffering. Jesus tended to the spiritual and physical needs of those around him. In watching Aunt Mary, I was reading the gospel of Christ without actually opening the Bible. In John 15:12–13, Jesus tells us, "My command is this: Love each other as I have loved you. Greater love has no one than this: to lay down one's life for one's friends" (NIV). Aunt Mary laid down her life for her family and her friends. The sacrifices she made taught me that one day I might have to do the same for someone in my family. If that time were to come, I would do so gladly and without complaint as though I was serving the Lord, just as Aunt Mary had done with Uncle Bunk.

Aunt Mary and her sister bring to mind two sisters who opened their home to Jesus as he traveled with his disciples. Those sisters were Mary and Martha from Luke 10. Both sisters loved Jesus but displayed that love in different ways. While the story is often interpreted as Jesus favoring one over the other, Scripture tells us that Jesus loved and appreciated them both (see John 11:5). Like Mary and Martha, Mama Hattie and Aunt Mary showed their love for Jesus in distinct ways, but they both exemplified the true love of God to our family and those around them.

Mama Hattie and Aunt Mary were important in the construction of my religious worldview, and it was during my experiences as a child in Rocky Mount, North Carolina, that this worldview was first formed. What a blessing it was for me to witness these two powerful women of God as a young Black girl. I was just a child, and my mind was developing its own understanding of the world around me. Without knowing it, somehow I was processing theological knowledge through the examples of Mama Hattie and Aunt Mary—Mama Hattie through her teaching me the Word of God directly and Aunt Mary through the example of her life of sacrifice. It was not until later that I realized that both modeled Christ's love right before my adolescent eyes.

"Because the Bible Tells Me So"

For many spiritual Black women and girls, our womanish exposure to the Bible came during moments with our mothers, grandmothers, or great-grandmothers. Even before being taught Scripture, we saw Bibles in the home that reminded us of the importance of the sacred text. In one conversation, my friend Angela reflected on her childhood: "We probably had one hundred Bibles in the house." Some of the Bibles in these homes had been passed down many generations. My mother still has the Bible that belonged to my great-grandmother, even with the pages withered and faded notes scrawled in the margins.

Educator Deborah De Sousa Owens writes, "The Bible is a sacred book to many Blacks. Black culture regards the Bible as a book that is to be treated with dignity and respect for it contains the words of an Almighty God. It has a distinct place of honor in many homes. Whether it is sitting on a mantel or a table, it is always handled with care. It is this kind of respect for the Bible and its content that forged a bond between Blacks generations ago."[5] Marnita Coleman writes that Bibles were much more than sacred writings, and that "some families still have family Bibles in the home that have served as a longstanding record for a growing family history."[6] Black girls who grew up with these Bibles in their homes knew at a young age that this text was blessed, holy, and not to be trifled with.

Scriptural artwork in many homes was also an expression of faith. Psalm 23 hung on the wall in some of our homes, reminding us that we should express full confidence and trust in the Lord and that God would provide all that we needed. These concrete displays provided us with a connection to the divine, even in a quick passing.

Black women's commitment to the Bible and its teachings has been passed down through generations. Our foremothers may not have been academy trained, but the wisdom gained through their life experiences qualified them as leading voices of the faith.

> *I mostly learned about faith from my grandma.—Danielle, 15*
>
> *My great-grandmother was an evangelist in the Church of God in Christ. My mom accepted her call to preach when I was in the second grade. We were a whole ministry family. —Trish, 39*

Katie Cannon, often acknowledged as a key figure in the establishment of the womanist movement, writes that her earliest thoughts of faith and ethics come from when she was a young Black girl listening to the wisdom and teaching of her grandmother.[7] Like womanist epistemology, woman*ish* epistemology is based in the oral culture passed down from those who came before us. In her essay "Marginalized People, Liberating Perspectives," Kelly Brown Douglas writes, "Existing on the margins of society and church provides a people with special epistemological advantage, a certain way of knowing, that is fundamental to creating a just society and church."[8] She goes on to suggest that these marginalized individuals have a distinctively insightful perspective on life because they rarely experience privilege yet still embody power and wisdom. Our foremothers realized their moral authority and responsibility in passing on Scripture to us as young Black girls. It is as though they wanted us to have something tangible to help us in our journey through life. The tradition of passing on Scripture to the next generation can be traced back to our painful history of slavery and the Christianization of African slaves. Africans resisted the slaveholders' use of the Bible to justify slavery and instead interpreted the text for themselves. Sharing personal interpretations of the Bible through oral storytelling or through music is how African Americans came to read the Bible for themselves.

Even if we as children failed to understand the nuances of the text, our foremothers encouraged us to commit specific passages to memory. One forty-three-year-old Black woman I spoke with could not remember Scripture study as a child, but Scripture memorization was a significant part of her upbringing. Among the Black women and girls I spoke with, Psalm 23, John 3:16, and Jeremiah 29:11 were mentioned most often as being memorized at young ages.

Memorizing John 3:16 is one of my earliest Scripture memories. I grew up memorizing verses, going to Vacation Bible School, having them plastered in the house or even in my room.

It was definitely a part of my home and church upbringing.
—Jacqueline, 14

I memorized Scripture early. I went to Vacation Bible School at my mother's church. All King James Version. Books of the Bible, I've known them since I was seven or eight. Whatever Mama said was the reason, I was okay with that.
—Deborah, 61

Memorizing Scripture was more important than interpreting it. It was like planting a seed that would grow within our souls. When the time came in life when we would be of need, our minds would access the sacred words for spiritual sustenance. This is a prescriptive approach to Scripture by which Black girls are taught that Scripture is instructive and medicinal. Growing up, I often heard Jeremiah 8:22: "Is there no balm in Gilead?" (NIV). The balm was interpreted as spiritual medicine.

We were also taught that Scripture instructs us in how we should live and behave and which commands to follow. Being taught Scripture on obedience was a paramount experience for Black girls growing up in spiritual households and churches. But using Scripture for behavior modification was complicated in the lives of many Black girls. Scripture passages reinforced the message that Black girls were not to "get out of line": obey your parents and you will live a long life (see Eph. 6:1–3), obey the Lord and keep God's commandments (see Deut. 30:16–20), and do everything without grumbling or complaining (see Phil. 2:14–15), are all unoffending messages at first glance, but when used for manipulation or control, they can be damaging to the Black girl hearing them.

Many Black girls, past and present, were introduced to Scripture through Bible story picture books or visual or audio means. Thirty-five-year-old Katherine loved the Bible growing up because her mother gave her Bible story cassettes that brought the Scriptures to life, and the two of them would listen together.

> *My mom bought me a coloring book on the book of Revelation as a kid. Crazy.—Destiny, 17*
>
> *I had something called* My Very First Bible. *It had David and Goliath, Adam and Eve, and Noah and the flood. That was how they introduced us to Scripture.—Michele, 14*
>
> *I had this Bible storybook that had Scriptures of Jesus's parables or stories that were dumbed down for kids. We talked about the concepts and the importance of the Word. My parents focused on Scriptures of Jesus. I took it as like these are a guideline of what I'm supposed to do for others in the world.—Imani, 15*

Sunday school and Vacation Bible School also exposed Black girls to Scripture. The importance of Vacation Bible School and Sunday school cannot be overstated. When Crystal was six, her Sunday school instructor taught her class how to find Scripture using a table of contents and how to use a concordance. The adults in her church wanted those who came behind them (the young people) to be prepared. Even as a thirty-year-old woman today, she is grateful for the trust the adult teachers had in them as young people. These teachers left impressions on Black girls as much as their schoolteachers. Crystal remembers her Sunday school teacher, Ms. Shayna, whom she loved and was drawn to. "I remember her reading John 15 to me once, and ever since then I have never let it go. As a girl, I thought to myself, *John 15 is going to be my Scripture*." Vacation Bible School was a significant part of my childhood and my teenage years. At my church, VBS was not only a place where I would see my friends, who had become like family, but also a place where we would spend a full week "in the Word," being equipped with Scripture and teaching that would help us to become stronger in our faith.

As young girls, most of us did not fully understand the sermons that were preached from the pulpit, but they were a way we were exposed to Scripture. Scripture is vital to a sermon. In my church, Scripture was read before the sermon, followed by the title of the sermon. Most of the time that was about all I caught growing up because the sermons were geared to more mature minds. That said, my pastor, Rev. "Buster" Soaries, would find other creative ways of teaching Scripture to the church. For one full year, in 1992, our church focused on Philippians 4:13. I remember vividly as a twelve-year-old walking into the sanctuary one day and seeing a huge yellow banner on the back wall with bold black letters that said, "I CAN DO ALL THINGS THROUGH CHRIST WHO STRENGTHENS ME." Rev. Soaries focused on Philippians 4:13 in all his sermons that year. Before he would preach, he would say, "I can!" The congregation would repeat after him, "I can!" The cycle would continue:

Pastor: "I can do!"
Congregation: "I can do!"
Pastor: "All things!"
Congregation: "All things!"
Pastor: "All things!"
Congregation: "All things!"
Pastor: "Through Christ"
Congregation: "Through Christ"
Pastor: "Who strengthens me"
Congregation: "Who strengthens me"
Pastor: "Amen."

This echoing happened almost every Sunday for the entire year. It took only a couple Sundays for me to know the Scripture passage by heart myself. Yet the focus didn't stop there. Philippians 4:13 was the verse for Sunday school classes all year and every program, event, and Bible study. We even had T-shirts with the passage on the front. In the summer my parents enrolled me in Vacation Bible School, and the focus of the week was Philippians 4:13. We sang songs, did Bible lessons, made crafts, and participated in activities based on the same Scripture passage. At the end of the week, every class made a presentation to all our families in a closing ceremony. Not only did we demonstrate that we had memorized Philippians 4:13 but we also shared what it meant to us. To me, it meant that I may not be able to do many things on my own, but with the help of Jesus I can do what seems impossible.

> *Exodus 20, I know that by heart because at my grandma's church we would recite it every Sunday. At Sunday school they would read it, and they would tell us what it was about. I feel like it's one thing for someone to tell you what you're reading and another for you to understand yourself. I want to understand what I'm reading.—Brandy, 17*

For the most part, Black girls are told to memorize Scripture and obey it. In reference to Scripture, one girl asked me, "How do you know what is right or what's real?" which is foundational to both exegesis and hermeneutics. We should teach Black girls not only to memorize Scripture but also to interpret it. We fail them when we skip the important step of teaching them context and meaning.

Many Black women recall that in their girlhood they were not empowered to judge biblical texts, and their adolescent minds were not trusted to offer biblical criticism. We did not get to point out the contradictions we saw or simply ask, "Why?" It wasn't until I started seminary that I was introduced to a hermeneutic of suspicion, a method of approaching Scripture with skepticism, thoughtfully and critically. Even then, as an adult, I was afraid to ask questions after being conditioned to just accept the text "as is." Forty-year-old Janice remembers not being able to question Scripture as a child: "If I said, 'Well, that doesn't make any sense,' or even when I connected the dots and it didn't make logical sense, they would push back and make it seem like I was questioning God. In reality, we were questioning Scripture. They just wanted us to read the book and that's it. We weren't invited to explore; we were just given."

Questioning Scripture as a child was like questioning God, something you don't do. We were taught Proverbs 9:10: "The fear of the LORD is the beginning of wisdom" (KJV). Questioning God was disrespectful. However, while we weren't invited to speak publicly about our questions, that did not mean we did not have them.

> *Sometimes I question because I grew up not eating pork because my mom said the Old Testament says not to do it. But then it also says don't mix your fabric, and we do that all the time. I have had to find things for my own, and I still question.—Alexa, 16*

Raven, in her early twenties, remembers learning about the Bible in church and thinking to herself, "*That doesn't make any sense. Last week you told us something else. That doesn't add up.* We were not always given room to explore the complications of Scripture." Raven says that in some ways this sent a message to us as young Black girls that our autonomy did not matter. It is possible that adults were trying to teach us things they did not always have the answers to. Questions would come from our inquisitive minds that some were not trained for. Still, they inadvertently taught us that pushing back or advocating for our thoughts was not allowed. Perhaps the fear was that our questions would lead us to lose the faith that adults had spent so much time teaching us. Perhaps they thought we would single out the contradictions and the flaws. Perhaps they thought we would identify the inaccuracies. Yet our questions did not need to be feared. Black girls can be trusted with biblical criticism just like adults.

> *I took a class called "Good and Evil" at school that taught a lot of different beliefs. I had a lot of questions going into that course, like "Why does evil happen?" or "Why did Adam and Eve happen?" I have always had a lot of questions, but I never doubted my faith. It was just like . . . I have a lot of questions.—Maya, 15*

Today many questions center around controversial interpretations of political and social issues, such as poverty, reproductive rights, women in leadership, and the treatment, experiences, and rights of those in the LGBTQ+ community. Many of the Black girls I interviewed either identify as a part of the LGBTQ+ community or are friends with others who do. When I asked them about any hang-ups they have with Scripture, it was clear that the treatment of the LGBTQ+ community is the main issue that turns them away from the church.

> *It should not matter who they love. They go by what their heart tells them.—Brooklyn, 17*
>
> *They have internalized homophobia.—Paige, 16*
>
> *Homosexuality is a big controversy among religious Christians. One day my grandma and I were watching a movie*

where there was a lesbian relationship, and she just leaned over and randomly asked me what I felt about that. I told her that love is love. She said the Bible says that you're not supposed to be a woman with another woman.—Latosha, 16

All my friends are gay, so I do not care. I remember telling my grandma that my friend Carson is trans, and she was dead silent. She gave me this look.—Aubri, 15

For Black girls, the act of loving one another is supreme. Love is above the controversial Scripture passages, and they loathe anything having to do with hate. I suppose they are the embodiment of what Jesus said is one of the greatest commandments, which is to love your neighbor as yourself.

Some families continue to share passages with Black girls even in their teenage years, whether they attend church or not. Their parents and grandparents pass on the importance of Scripture as prescriptive for their lives. To these adults, Scripture is authoritative and provides guidance for how Black girls should behave and make decisions.

"My mom, she sends me verses every morning," Destiny says.

"That's like my mom! And my dad," Imani adds begrudgingly.

"Bruh, my grandma just sent me Scriptures just now," Michele adds.

The girls and I get a laugh from their shared experiences.

"What's App," Destiny continues. "My mom sends the Scripture with pictures. It's like thousands." She shows me the picture on the screen. It says, "Goodnight. Psalm 27:1."

In unison, the girls recite the passage: "The Lord is my light and my salvation; whom shall I fear? The Lord is the strength of my life; of whom shall I be afraid?" (KJV).

"Every morning!" Destiny exclaims. "Ugh!"

I know the girls secretly appreciate their families' texts. It's their way of showing the girls they love them and continuing the tradition of instilling in them the importance of Scripture and showing them how Scripture is essential to their growth and maturity. Receiving the Scripture text messages from their families is really no different from my brother, cousins, and I reading Scripture before every meal around the table in the dining room. Scripture was instilled in me by Mama Hattie and lived out before my eyes in Aunt Mary. Scripture was nurtured in me at my church, in Sunday school, and in Vacation Bible School. This same Scripture would follow me all the days of my life as I continued to journey in my own faith and spirituality.

Receiving a Torch

After Uncle Bunk died in 2012, my mother and aunts decided to sell the family home and move Aunt Mary up north to live with Aunt Jane, where she would be until her death in 2023. When Aunt Mary died, I drove to Rocky Mount to meet my family and lay to rest our family matriarch. To my surprise, things seemed to be the way they were all those years ago. The Belk Department Store was still there, just with an upgraded look. The Piggly Wiggly and Gardner's Barbeque Restaurant were still there. We even gathered at the old Ebenezer Baptist Church for the funeral, and the building looked as good as new.

As we walked into the church, we were greeted by all the familiar people the Clark family had known for decades and who I remembered only by the associations I'd created for them as a child. There was Larry Bird (not to be confused with the Hall of Fame basketball player), my aunt Toxi's high school sweetheart. There was Ms. Pam, who made all the scratch cakes and brought them over to the house when we were in town. There was Mr. Charlie, who always made chopped barbeque, and Tyrone, a close friend we called a cousin. They were all there because they all knew and loved Aunt Mary and my family.

To my surprise, Rev. Walker was there, just a bit older and frailer. He offered a final eulogy to her of kind words and thoughts of their friendship for the past fifty years and sang his signature song, "One Day at a Time," which I never imagined my adult ears would have the chance to hear live again.

After the service was over, before heading to the cemetery, the procession of cars drove past the house on Powell Drive one last time. I drove my car, and my siblings rode with me. We listened to Kirk Franklin songs and marveled at all the landmarks we remembered from childhood. As we slowly pulled up to the old one-story, brick house, my childhood flashed before my eyes, and I was overcome with quiet emotion. I would not be who I am today if not for Mama Hattie, Aunt Mary, and Ma Rosella, who offered up their lives for me and my family. My heart burst with gratitude as I remembered that this was where my faith began. When we arrived at the cemetery, we walked past the gravestones of Mama Hattie and Ma Rosella. My family made sure Aunt Mary would be buried near where they were laid to rest. I was asked to offer final words. It felt like receiving a torch to carry on what Mama Hattie and Aunt Mary had taught me, to carry on the faith on their behalf. As I stood before our family and friends, I had the pleasure of offering the committal prayer:

> *What a gift. What an honor that God allowed us . . . that God trusted us to experience such a special love in our lifetime. As now we offer Aunt Mary back into God's arms, may God comfort us in our loneliness, may God strengthen us in our weakness and give us courage to face the future unafraid. And to Aunt Mary, as she enters eternity, may she hear the words "Well done, thy good and faithful servant." Amen.*

2

Woman*ish* Theology of Salvation

How Black Girls Get "Saved"

When my family moved from Brooklyn to New Jersey in the early 1990s, their first goal was to find a church. We were active members of a historic church in Brooklyn that we loved and where I had been dedicated as a child, so it was essential that we find a similar church in New Jersey. At a baby dedication, the parents and the church commit to raise the child in a godly way until the child is old enough to make their own decisions, and they ask God to bless and guide the child as that child grows. There are pictures of me being dedicated as a baby in an all-white gown as I am held by my dad and surrounded by my mom and my godmother, Aunt Cathy. The pastor of Brooklyn's Bethany Baptist Church, civil rights leader William Augustus Jones Jr., was a big deal during that time, so looking back I consider my beginnings in church predictive of my life journey into ministry and justice work.

As my parents searched for a New Jersey church, it was important to them that the church was both active in the community and Bible-based, which means it emphasized the Bible as the standard of faith and practice. My parents heard about a church not far from our new home that we visited and ultimately joined: First Baptist Church of Lincoln Gardens in Somerset, New Jersey. Like other historic Black churches, First Baptist was a dominant institutional force in its surrounding community. As at Bethany Baptist, we became active members of the church, and I grew up attending Sunday morning services with my parents and brother.

Each Sunday, after Rev. Buster Soaries finished preaching, he would extend an invitation for individuals to commit their lives to Christ for the first time, join the church as a member, or renew their membership if they'd been away or had not been active at the church for some time. This moment was known as "the invitation." People were invited to respond to the gospel that had been preached and make a conscious commitment to Christ in their mind and heart. We saw this as the moment a person decided to "get saved."

My entire life I have heard that phrase, as in "When did you get saved?" Most Christians immediately understand, but for the nonreligious person, it can be confounding. For a young person, religious or not, the concept of "getting saved" is as weighty in meaning as in practice. As a young girl, I knew it was a major decision, a lifelong commitment, and not to be taken lightly.

I was ten years old when I decided to officially give my life to Christ. Pastor Soaries had finished his sermon and extended the invitation as usual. I can't recall if this was preplanned or on a whim, but my parents were aware that I was to go up. In that moment, I walked up to the front of the church on my own. I was greeted by one of the deacons, who sat with me in the front and asked me a few important questions. I do not remember them all, but I do know they asked me if I believed that Jesus Christ died for my sins, was resurrected, and is coming back again. I answered yes to all the questions. After Pastor Soaries was done with his invitation, he came down from the pulpit and went to each person who had come forward, and the deacon or deaconess said our name and what we had come forward for. My doting parents looked on with emotion and joy as I stood with the deacon who told the congregation that I had come forward to give my life to Christ. The congregation erupted in applause. Pastor Soaries then prayed for us, and I went back to my parents in the pew. After church, we sat in the new members' room, and the deacons went over instructions on what would take place before I got baptized. I would have to complete a series of new believers' classes to learn what it means to be a follower of Jesus.

In those classes, I learned that baptism is one of the two New Testament ordinances (or sacraments) of the church, the other being the Lord's Supper, which is also referred to as Communion. I'd always known of the importance of Communion because Mama Hattie wouldn't let me take it when I'd sit with her at Ebenezer Baptist. I had to be "saved" to take Communion. Baptism, I learned, is a commission of the church. Matthew 28:19 says, "Go ye therefore, and teach all nations, baptizing them in the name of the Father, and of the Son, and of the Holy Ghost" (KJV). Baptism solidified my commitment and my salvation. I learned about sin, prayer, and other spiritual disciplines. I also learned the church covenant and what it means. Every first Sunday of the month, before believers would take Communion, we would read the church covenant aloud. I still know it by heart to this day.

Preacher: What experience defines our spiritual fellowship and covenant relationship?
Congregation: Having been led, as we believe, by the Spirit of God, to receive the Lord Jesus as our Savior and on the profession of our faith, having been baptized in the name of the Father, and of the Son, and of the Holy Spirit, we do now in the presence of God and this assembly, most solemnly and joyfully enter into covenant with one another as one body in Christ.

Preacher: What is the bond of our union?
Congregation: By grace through faith, we are saved. We are a chosen people, a royal priesthood, a holy nation.

Preacher: What tasks do we assume as the people of God?
Congregation: To go and to teach all nations, baptizing them in the name of the Father, and of the Son, and of the Holy Spirit: teaching them to observe all that Christ commands.

Preacher: To what lifestyle and conversation are we pledged?
Congregation: To do goodness, love mercy, and walk humbly before our God. To love the Lord God with all our hearts, minds, souls, and strength, and to love our neighbors as ourselves.

It amazes me that I recited these deeply theological and mature statements as a child. I had little understanding of what these words meant, but the class taught me that I had a responsibility to Christ and to my church, and those are principles that never left me. When I was finished with the new believers' classes, I was ready to be baptized.

The week leading to my baptism, I practiced dunking my head in the bathtub, though admittedly I knew that our bathtub at home wasn't nearly as deep as the church baptismal pool was. I dunked forward even though I knew Pastor Soaries would bring me down into the water backward. Thoughts raced in my head. How long would I be held down? Would I drown if he held me down too long? What about my hair? I was nervous.

The day of the baptism, my mom walked me to the side room where all the candidates gathered. I had to change into a white gown, and thankfully I had a swim cap that would protect my hair from getting wet. Most of the parents dropped off their kids and went into the main area to watch the baptism, but my mom was a deaconess in the church, so she had special privileges. The deaconesses gathered us to pray together, and then we got in line as the service started. Our church baptisms did not take place in the sanctuary because the baptismal pool was in the basement, and the ceremony was not during a typical Sunday service but on a separate weekend day and time. I do not remember much about the service because I was so nervous and focused on making sure I remembered to hold my breath so that I did not drown.

The basement was also known as our fellowship hall. The space was old and charmless, a multipurpose room that hosted many activities and gatherings. The pool was adjacent to the fellowship hall behind a divider that concealed it from the area. As I stood in line, I watched the candidates before me, young and old, go one at a time to a room full of joyful family and friends. Pastor Soaries stood in the baptism pool, and Deacon Jones and Deacon Presley stood at the stairs to help each of the candidates down into the pool. One of the deacons sang, "Take me to the waaaater. Take me to the waaaater. Take me to the waaaater, to be baptized."[1] The candidate in front of me stepped down into the pool, and I moved forward. I was even more nervous. This was the moment my life was going to change. Was I going to *feel* like a new person when I came up out of the water? I had heard time and time again that I was going to come up new, but I did not understand that this was more internal than external. The deacon then called my name: "Khristi Adams."

I nervously and slowly walked down the steps of the pool, and Pastor Soaries was there to meet me. The water was surprisingly warm and inviting.

Pastor: "Khristi, have you made a decision to follow Jesus and live your life only for him?"

I nodded my head yes.

Pastor: "Parents, will you do your best to provide support to Khristi in her faith and spiritual journey?"

My parents said yes.

Pastor: "Do you, the members of this congregation, in the name of Jesus, promise to welcome Khristi into the family of God and to encourage her to grow as a disciple of Jesus Christ?"

Enthusiastically, members of the congregation who were in attendance said yes.

Pastor: "With this profession of faith, Khristi, I baptize you in the name of the Father, the Son, and the Holy Ghost."

I closed my eyes tight and held my breath, and he leaned me back into the warm water. The water rushed over my head, and in what felt like the blink of an eye, I was standing on my feet. It was over. I was made new, as they said. Even as a ten-year-old, I knew this moment was significant.

Salvation, Sanctification, and Sin

When I ask a Black woman or Black girl who either identifies as Christian or grew up in a Christian family, "When did you get saved?" they almost always know exactly what I mean. I am fascinated by how young Black girls are expected to process the phrase "get saved." Daniel Migliore writes, "The Greek term *soteria* is translated 'salvation' and means rescue from mortal peril, deliverance from sin and death, and the gift of fulfilled life in communion with God."[2] Within the Christian tradition, salvation is obtained through Jesus Christ. In Protestantism, salvation can be interpreted in many ways. In the Black church tradition, however, when we speak of getting saved, we are typically referring to one single event or moment.

Many womanist theologians emphasize a holistic approach to salvation, which includes liberation from oppression and injustice on multiple fronts, such as racism, sexism, classism, and other forms of discrimination. Salvation, from a womanist perspective, is not solely about individual spiritual salvation but also about the collective liberation of marginalized communities. Womanist theology suggests that salvation is also a path to liberation from the oppression and suffering that Black women have faced. For many Black girls, however, our introduction to salvation was typically within the traditional definition, without salvation necessarily speaking into our marginalized identities.

At its core, salvation is a complex doctrine for a Black girl to understand. We were told that we needed to be saved from sin (another difficult concept) and that the consequence of sin is death. We were told that there is only one name under heaven by which human beings can be saved, which is Jesus Christ. In my young mind, I understood sin as being bad; therefore, we needed deliverance from it, or we would likely go to hell.

Our church was talking about Revelation a lot. And I remember hearing that if we didn't get saved, we would go to hell. I was in first or second grade, and all I kept thinking was that I did not want to go to hell. I got saved because I was afraid of hell. I was only five years old.—Rhyanne, 28

Sin, death, heaven, and hell are complicated concepts to understand at such young ages! Of the Black women and girls I spoke with, the ones who did "get saved" were as young as six years old when they made the decision to accept Christ. For the most part, when thinking back to their moment of getting saved, they often recall their baptism, because in many Black churches, baptism is a condition of salvation.[3] The messaging was vague at times because we were told that baptism was important but not necessary for salvation, but we still had to do it, so to me they were one and the same. This is the reason I believe most Black girls' salvation narratives center on baptism.

I got baptized between the age of five and seven. The preacher said, "Who wants to be baptized? Who's not saved?" A bunch of kids stood up. He asked each of us why we wanted to be baptized.—Nicole, 30

I was baptized at eleven. It wasn't planned. Sometimes they plan baptisms. But it was my choice, and I knew what I was doing. To me, baptism was what was preached and taught. When you go under the water, you come up as a new self. I really resonated with that. But sometimes as a child, it's not your own faith; it's your family's. For me, this was a step I took into actually taking my faith seriously.—Talisa, 14

I got baptized pretty young, but I wasn't really saved until middle school. "Saved" to me meant that I had a relationship with God. When I got baptized, I was young and I thought that this was what I was supposed to do, but it's not until I got older that I understood what that meant.—Sharon, 30

Getting saved from death with a goal of heaven was not the only motivation for getting saved. If we grew up within a community of Christians, we wanted to be accepted into the group and did not want to feel left out. That is not to take away from the gravity of our personal decision, but our context certainly played a role.

> *I was seven when I got saved. Now that I look back on it, I think I went up because I saw my best friend go up. But I knew I loved Jesus and that going up was a feeling like this is what I'm supposed to be doing. It was the end of the church service, and they asked if anyone wanted to go up, and I asked my mom if I could go, and she had tears in her eyes. It wasn't until I was in the classes that I really started to digest that I made a really adult decision. But I was proud of myself.—Jade, 30*

I got baptized at age ten. Despite our young age or other factors that may have led us to get saved, most of our families and churches were intentional in teaching us about the meaning of salvation and baptism before we were baptized. One woman shared that her mom always told her that when it came to baptism, she needed to be able to articulate why she wanted to get baptized. This was the case with many of us. Because of this, I can say with confidence that I did know what I was doing. Sometimes as adults, we assume that young people's minds are incapable of retaining meaningful knowledge. However, I believe that Black girls have an innate wisdom that gives them the ability to absorb the information and experiences they are exposed to at young ages.

If someone doesn't want to be saved, you don't need to give them anxiety about the fact that they didn't. If they need time to process and repent before they make the decision, then it's up to them.—Elana, 15

My friend Ebonee vividly recalls her moment of salvation at age seven. She had a conversation with her parents, who were adamant that it should be her own decision. When she decided to get saved, like many of us, she walked to the front of the church and said the sinner's prayer with a deacon. It amazes me that so many of us who grew up in the church have similar stories but also that we understood the seriousness of our decision.

Sometimes as a child in church, you're there but it's not really your own faith because it's the family's. That's what you do. But this was a step I took into actually taking my faith seriously.—Kim, 15.

I have learned and believe you're saved when you believe that Jesus died for our sins. He gives us the gift of being able to go to heaven, and it's our choice whether we want to accept that gift. But we also should have our own relationship or do our devotionals. We want to be able to connect to Jesus. For me, salvation is a gift, and I have to accept it for myself.—Anna, 14

After my baptism, I never questioned my salvation. I knew I'd made a lifelong commitment and thought that I was now officially going to get into heaven. When I got saved, I thought it was a one-time decision and act. I was confused at times as to why anyone would need to rededicate their life to Christ when the pastor offered that invitation from the pulpit. I typically ignored that part of the altar call, as it was always quick, but a few years after my baptism, the idea of our need to sustain our salvation was brought to my attention. The theological concept of eternal security means that once a person is saved, they are always saved. It wasn't until our church's youth ministry took a trip to a youth conference in 1994 that I began to question salvation. Could a believer lose their salvation? How? Why?

Our youth ministry took a group of teens and preteens to Washington, DC, for a five-day conference called DC '94.[4] The first conference was called DC '91, but in 1991 I was too young to attend, so I was elated when the opportunity presented itself again. In 1994 I was twelve and a half, so I just made the cutoff. I did not know what the conference would entail but was hyped to be on the bus with the older kids I looked up to. Some twenty thousand youth from all over the country attended the conference at the Washington Convention Center. There was a host of speakers, concerts featuring Christian artists, and workshops that our youth leaders and chaperones escorted us to. I was amazed that there were so many youths and that so many of them were White. We were from one of the few Black churches represented, but we did not feel weird about it because we stayed together the entire trip, eating meals, socializing, and attending different sessions.

The focus of DC '94 was "True Love Waits." This was a campaign to get teenagers to promise to wait until marriage to have sex. I did not know much of anything about sex. I just kept hearing the message that it was bad, and we weren't supposed to do it.[5] I did not understand what that had to do with my salvation, however. The message at that conference was that many of us needed to rededicate our lives to Christ by deliberately rejecting sin, and in this case, the sin of even thinking about sex. To me, the call to recommit our lives meant that the first time I committed my life wasn't good enough. I needed to get saved *again*. In one of the main sessions, the speaker delivered his message, and when he was finished, volunteers stood up and handed cards to us to fill out. The cards were pledge cards, and if we signed, we were promising that we would not have sex until we were married. I did not know the layers to what I was signing. All I knew was that it was bad to have sex or to think about having sex and that I needed to sign to let God know that I wouldn't. After we signed, the pastor called students forward who wanted to rededicate their lives to Christ. Thousands of students crowded to the front of the altar to repeat the sinner's prayer:

> *Dear Jesus, I know I am a sinner, and I ask for your forgiveness. I believe you died for my sins and rose from the dead. I turn from my sins and invite you to come into my heart and life. You are my Lord and Savior, and I give my life to you again. Amen.*

I could sigh a sigh of relief. I was saved again. Yet the moment set a dangerous precedent for me. I would spend many days afterward attempting to evade sin (especially anything sexual in nature) so that I would not lose my salvation. Any opportunity I had to rededicate my life I took as a means of wiping the slate of sin clean so that my salvation could be restored. I did not realize that the doctrine of salvation involved God redeeming humankind. My salvation came through faith in Christ only. While this did not exempt me from human transgressions in the form of sin, I did not need to get saved again. I was saved.

> *Basically, you're telling me I'm a bad person and I need to live for God to be a good person. It's a challenging concept for the young mind.—Porsha, 17*

A theology of salvation is complicated because the saved individual is supposed to be saved from sin and death, but the continual presence of the sins of everyday transgressions can easily lead a person to question their salvation. Migliore writes that "the New Testament speaks of salvation in past, present, and future tenses: we 'have been saved' (Eph. 2:8); we 'are being saved' (1 Cor. 15:2); and we 'shall be saved' (Rom. 5:10)."[6] The "are being saved" notion speaks to sanctification, which is "the process of 'being made holy.'"[7] Sanctification is a theological concept that refers to the ongoing transformation of believers to become more Christlike in their character and conduct. I'd always heard the word *sanctified* growing up, and I knew that it was important for me to evolve in my faith, but I was not adequately taught about sanctification, which is why I so often confused it with salvation. When I was a young person, concepts like salvation, sanctification, and sin always seemed to jumble together. I needed to be saved and sanctified, but I wasn't sure if I was still saved if I sinned. Some Christians focus their attention on sin, and somehow salvation becomes contingent on the type and sum of sins. Some Black girls take issue with this.

I sat with a small group of teenage girls at a youth retreat, and we had a conversation about their views on religion and salvation. I could sense their frustration with the attention Christians give to certain sins.

"I don't get it," Sona said. "It's always sex. Like those billboards that say, 'Shackled by lust? Jesus sets you free.'"

"That's the billboard I see on the way to school every day!" Arianna exclaimed.

"We don't have those up north," Sharifa stated, "but I mean I get it. It's like when Jesus saves me, he only saves me from anything having to do with sex."

"Like what's that celebrity's name? Blac Chyna? She's *finally* been saved," Sona continued. "When she did her salvation, everybody was like 'She's finally cured from all the bad stuff she's been doing,' and I was like hold on. She's going through her own thing and she's talking about how she was saved by Jesus, not that she's doing this for you all. She got all her fillers out, and she got baptized."

Ryia added to Sona's thoughts. "Yeah, people are like 'She's finally been saved.' Like 'finally' is a big word. She's a daughter of God. So, she wasn't a daughter of God before? They say God loves her *again*. Isn't God's love supposed to be eternal?"

"I think she was a Christian before," Arianna responded. "She just didn't exemplify it the way people thought she should." (She emphasized the word *should* with air quotes.)

Angela Renee White, a.k.a. Blac Chyna, was known for her lavish lifestyle and being a sexually liberated woman. In 2023 she revealed that she was giving up that way of living and was on a new spiritual path. The headlines read, "Blac Chyna Says That Finding Christ Made Her Quit OnlyFans," "Blac Chyna Gets Baptized and Removes Tattoo," and "Did Blac Chyna Receive Her Salvation?" White made visible changes to her appearance, removing tattoos, losing weight, reversing previous plastic surgeries, and shying away from anything sexual. To the girls I spoke with, White was saved before, and they resented that anyone would question her salvation based on her lifestyle changes. If she was a believing Christian before, perhaps she was now in the "are being saved" part of her salvation. Perhaps she was merely exhibiting sanctification in public.

"It's like when you're saved, you're not doing any of that anymore. So then when they start doing it, does that mean that they're not saved?" Riya asked.

"It depends on the person if they feel saved or not. Everybody makes mistakes," Sona said.

"I think of salvation as something that is personal. It's a personal journey for you. It's your thing."

I get the sense that Black girls do understand salvation to be the start of a journey. There are steps to that journey, but one is no more or less "saved" depending on what stage of the journey they're in.

I think getting saved is more of a process. I think getting saved means you're now following Christ and you start the journey.—Mel, 17

God saved me out of my depressive state or my suicidal thoughts or addictions that I had. When God saved me, he saved me from myself and my hole. Salvation is about heaven, yes, but it also saved me from the sin of being in my own prison.—Carissa, 16

As long as they believe and have their own understanding with God, then it's not up to me to judge if they're saved or not.—Niche, 13

At the same time, to some salvation is more than just words. Fourteen-year-old Alicia says, "A lot of people will 'get saved' and nothing happens because you can say the words and then not go back and pursue God at all." However, some Black girls are adamant that how a person decides to pursue God is up to them. As much as they appreciate their families passing on the faith, they don't want anyone telling them what faith is and how it should feel. They want to experience it for themselves. For the girls who have been taught about faith yet feel disconnected from it, spirituality can feel distant. "I've been told my whole life what it is," fifteen-year-old Jess says, "but now I want to feel it and I don't." Others struggle with committing to believing in something so specific. Jess goes on to ask, "How do you know what's going to happen when you die? If you put your faith in something for such a long time and it turns out not to be true, that would be such a waste of time." Yet Black girls don't necessarily question faith and salvation as concepts, and they understand both to be deeply personal.

> *In all my confusion with Christianity and faith, the one thing I am solid on is salvation. I have seen what rock-solid faith is. I don't have any questions about salvation except How do I get there? How do I get to that point? I see people and they have this deep faith, and I'm like something in your life that you experienced was so revolutionary that what you believe now is your center, your core, and your anchor. I haven't had that.—Katrina, 18*

Once Saved, Always Saved

Later in my teenage years, I made a spur-of-the-moment decision to get baptized again. I was away at a youth retreat, where I could socialize with friends, but it was also a time of deep reflection, worship, and prayer. Toward the end of the retreat, the youth leader, Pastor Matt, gave us an opportunity to recommit our lives to Christ. Not only could we do this through prayer, but there was also a pool where we could get baptized. Some of my peers had never been baptized, so in that moment they decided to. I'd already been baptized and wasn't sure if I should do it again. Would my baptism count more this time, now that I was more cognizant of what I was doing? A rush of emotions came over me, and I stood up to say that I wanted to be baptized.

Pastor Matt called me into the pool and asked the standard questions about whether I believed in Jesus Christ. He added a few things that were different from my first baptism, about living a life that was holy. I agreed to it all. When I went into the pool this time, I was not scared of the water; I welcomed it. The few people there clapped, and I walked out to grab my towel. I did not feel any different this time. I felt nothing.

Immediately, I started to question why I got baptized again. For some reason, I thought this would somehow legitimize the first baptism. This time I *knew* what I was doing. I believe I questioned whether I knew what I was doing as a ten-year-old because as I became more spiritually mature, I concluded that my childhood faith was not enough. But looking back, I think of Matthew 18:3. When the disciples ask Jesus, "Who is the greatest in the kingdom of heaven?" he responds, "Truly I tell you, unless you change and become like little children, you will never enter the kingdom of heaven" (NIV).

Had I accepted this childlike faith, I would have counted my first baptism as sufficient. In that moment, soaking wet from the pool, I decided that I would not get baptized again. My salvation, my faith, and my baptism when I initially gave my life to Christ as a ten-year-old were more than enough. I was more than enough.

Womanish Theology of the *Imago Dei*

How Black Girls Embody the Image of God

I, too, sing America.

I am the darker brother.
They send me to eat in the kitchen
When company comes,
But I laugh,
And eat well,
And grow strong.

Tomorrow,
I'll be at the table
When company comes.
Nobody'll dare
Say to me,
"Eat in the kitchen,"
Then.

Besides,
They'll see how beautiful I am
And be ashamed—

I, too, am America.[1]

As a six-year-old, I was tasked with reciting this 1926 poem written by Langston Hughes at my kindergarten graduation at Brooklyn Junior Academy. My teacher, Ms. Mumford, set high expectations for us and was known to be a strict disciplinarian. When the time came for graduation, we had an opportunity to show our families how much we had grown and learned over the course of the school year. Ms. Mumford taught us writing and arithmetic and introduced us to Black historical figures, Black art, and Black writers. Hughes was one such writer, and "I, Too" was more than a poem to recite. It was a declaration for us as Black children being sent off into a society that didn't always see us as beautiful. By having me recite the poem, Ms. Mumford added the nuance of a young female voice speaking the words, and I substituted "I am the darker brother" with "I am the darker sister."

In the days leading up to graduation, I said the lines repeatedly with my mother and practiced them at school with Ms. Mumford so that I did not just recite the words but projected them with confidence. When graduation came, I belted out, "I am the darker sister!" No truer words had been spoken of who I was aesthetically, and no truer words prophesied how I would struggle in the world as a darker sister in the years to come. My experiences reconciling my Black identity with my faith are fundamentally related to the concepts and ideas that are a part of my spiritual worldview and that I have developed in my theological work.

I was born in Brooklyn in the 1980s in a time when the borough was filled mostly with Black faces. I saw the world through living in a community surrounded by Black people and never considered the world through any other lens. My parents put me in programs and activities with other Black kids, I went to a Black Baptist church, and I went to a school called Junior Academy, a private educational institution for Black children. On the playground, I participated in Black girlhood practices that were important to my identity, like double Dutch, a game with two long jump ropes in which two or more girls jump in between the ropes at the same time. I got my hair cornrowed and braided in different styles, an inextricable part of Black culture. My friends and I would admire each other's barrettes and beads, which were usually sealed by putting small pieces of aluminum foil at the ends to keep the beads from falling out. I played hand-clapping games with my best friend, Taysia, and our other friends on the concrete playground during recess. We'd sing,

> Uno, dos-ee-ay-say Said east, west,
> met my boyfriend at the candy store.
> He brought me ice cream, he brought me cake,
> he brought me home with a belly ache.
> Mama, mama, I'm so sick,
> call the doctor quick, quick, quick!

Doctor, doctor, will I die?
Just close your eyes and count to five!

These rites and practices were a significant part of shaping my identity. They were how my world was shaped until my family moved to New Jersey when I was in the second grade. Only after we moved did I become acutely aware of how I took up space in the world. We moved from an apartment in Brooklyn to a house in a suburb in East Brunswick. I was initially very excited to be in a new community and to meet new friends at a new school. We were the only Black family in the neighborhood. I remember being cognizant of the fact that there was something different about us as a family in the all-White community that we lived in, but the people in the community embraced us as any other new family.

It was not until I started school that this difference hit me like a ton of bricks.

In my book *Parable of the Brown Girl*, I write about my first day at Frost Elementary School:

> It seemed there were hundreds and hundreds of students. *And these students looked nothing like me.* I was confused and overwhelmed, and I could not find one person who looked like me. I was lost. My young mind couldn't process what was happening. Though I felt very different, I still tried to make connections with the people around me. I tried to join in by playing with two white boys on the playground. One was happy to hang out with me, the other protested, "We don't play with n*ggers," already

> comfortable and conditioned to use racist language. Other students asked uncomfortable questions like, "Why does your skin get like that?" or "Why does your hair shrivel up like that?" or "Can you tan?"[2]

"Get out of here, darky!" I distinctly remember a classmate screaming at me when I wanted to join their group in class. In East Brunswick, suddenly my Black body was a problem. My hair was a problem that needed to be tamed. That was the moment I, as a Black girl in a White world, was introduced to the White gaze, which rendered both my ethnicity and my gender invisible. Up until that point, I was shielded from how Whiteness dominates how society operates and how people think. Growing up in Brooklyn, I was merely a Black girl in a Black world. In East Brunswick, I was a Black girl in a White world, and it impacted how I viewed myself for years to come.

My parents kept me active in extracurriculars. I was one of two Black girls in my dance class, and when picture time came and the teacher ordered nude stockings for us, I was the only girl with beige stockings up against dark skin because my Black classmate had a much lighter skin tone. The instrument I chose to learn for orchestra was the violin, and I was always the only Black girl in those settings. Yet I found solidarity and safety with the many Asian students in the orchestra. My mom signed me up for the local Girl Scout troop, where I was also the only Black girl. I distinctly remember one camping trip when I watched the White girls sharing shampoo while we took showers before our evening campfire and movie.

Not wanting to feel left out, I asked to share the bottle and lathered my hair the same way they had done. When I got out of the shower, my hair did not return to the straight tresses that my mother had spent hours hot combing to prepare for the trip. While the girls watched the movie, I sat in another room while my mom worked to comb and braid my hair. I was humiliated. It did not matter where I went in those spaces. I could not escape that my Black aesthetic was a problem. Thank God my parents were adamant about the Black church being a significant part of my upbringing and lifestyle. Simply attending church was helpful to shaping my identity as a Black girl and as the *imago Dei* (image of God).

Preparing to go to church on Sunday mornings was a ritual of Black pride and dignity. My mom would put out my church dress the night before. She would iron it and hang it up so that it would be ready to put on in the morning. My hair was also a priority—especially if it was Easter Sunday or another sacred day on the church calendar. If I didn't visit the beauty salon on Saturday, my mom would prepare my hair herself the night before. When I was younger and spent summers in Rocky Mount, North Carolina, the night before church my grandmother would press my hair with a hot comb because my coarse hair wasn't permed yet and needed to be straightened. Mama Hattie would put the hot comb on the electric stove to heat up. When it was ready, I would tilt my head to the side and hold my ear down so that I did not get burned. When we lived in New Jersey, my hair was permed straight, so we could skip the hot comb part, unless my kinky roots had grown in. Then my mom would use a hot comb on my roots so they matched the rest of my straight hair. I loved to wear my hair down, which meant that it was straight and to my shoulders, sometimes with a big curl at the ends that we called a "bump." Sometimes I wore my hair in cornrows with beads at the end, in box braids or microbraids, slicked back into a bun, or in two ponytails with spiral curls. The possibilities for my Black hair were endless. I loved going to church and seeing my friends in their different hairstyles too! Black hair culture was a part of my Black identity. That part of myself was not appreciated at the White school I attended, but at First Baptist, Black culture and identity were deeply embedded into church culture. They were one and the same.

My family all dressed in their "Sunday best"—my mom in her usual chic and classic style and my dad in his best tailored suit. My brother always had on a suit that looked like our dad's. When we got to church, we walked in among other Black families with their own versions of their Sunday best outfits, which often included suits, dresses, hats, and accessories. How we looked wasn't about money or flaunting socioeconomic backgrounds but instead was a way we demonstrated respect for the church, the congregation, and the act of worship itself. It was a way to honor God by presenting ourselves in our finest attire as a reflection of our gratitude and commitment to our faith. It wasn't until later in life that I connected our tradition of dressing for church to the *imago Dei*. The *imago Dei* is about dignity and value. It means that every individual possesses inherent dignity and worth because they reflect the divine image. In the *imago Dei*, all human life is sacred and deserving of respect. This was undoubtedly what we aimed to express when we presented ourselves as our aesthetically best on Sunday mornings. We were essentially expressing that we too are the *imago Dei*.

First Baptist Church helped form my identity simply because it was a Black church with Black people who looked like me. When I looked to the pulpit on Sunday mornings, I saw both men and women sitting in leadership positions. To me, Black women standing in the pulpit, wearing ministerial robes, leading services, and boldly preaching the Word of God was the standard. One Sunday, as she was leading the congregation in a hymn, Rev. Johnson repeatedly replaced the pronoun "he" for God with "she," and everyone kept singing awkwardly. I laughed nervously with one of my friends next to me in the pew. I could not understand why she would do that but thought it daring and bold. Even an act as seemingly small as replacing a pronoun in a hymn shaped my theology. These women in positions of influence served as my role models and were critical to my own career and vocational advancement. They were also essential to my theology—a theology that identifies with women's leadership, gifts, and unique callings.

Still, there were times even in church when I experienced the plight of my dark skin and Black body. While I experienced racism in my White school, I experienced colorism in predominantly Black spaces like my church. I distinctly remember when a church member asked my mother if I was adopted simply because my skin was a darker brown than my mother's. I remember sitting in a room of peers after choir rehearsal one day and hearing one of my brother's friends say, "I could never date a dark-skinned girl." Then he leaned over to me and said, "No offense, Khristi."

On rare occasions, Song of Songs was quoted from the pulpit or in Christian education settings. I believe we heard it only rarely because of its sensual language, although some saw the book as representative of God's abiding love for God's people. A traditional interpretation is that the book tells a story of two lovers: Solomon and the Shulamite. It is suggested that the Shulamite woman is a dark-skinned woman, perhaps of African descent. The Shulamite woman speaks early in chapter 1. We were a New King James Version church, so I heard her say,

> I am dark, but lovely,
> O daughters of Jerusalem,
> Like the tents of Kedar,
> Like the curtains of Solomon.
> Do not look upon me, because I am dark. (Song 1:5–6)

Other versions have "Dark and lovely" or "Black and beautiful." As a Black girl, I felt both seen and confused when I first heard this. "Dark and lovely" or "dark *but* lovely"? "Black and beautiful" or "Black *but* beautiful"? I'd heard something similar before when a boy at church said that I was "pretty for a dark-skinned girl." The fact of the matter is that I was dark in complexion and that my darkness always seemed to come with a "but."

I was determined to solve the problem of my dark skin. I tried my hardest to steer clear of being directly in the sun, and I looked forward to the winter months, when there was less sun exposure and decreased melanin production. Trips to the grocery store or pharmacy with my parents always included going to the skincare aisle to look for Ambi Skin Cream. Ambi was advertised to "gradually fade dark areas for even natural skin tone," and while the product itself was for dark spots and discolorations, in my young mind, the entirety of my dark complexion was the discoloration. I would apply the cream to my face at night and wake up in the morning to see if it had lightened my skin. The cream never did change my skin tone, but I'd convinced myself that it was doing something because that's what the label promised. When my skin did not lighten fast enough, I thought that lightening my hair would be the next best option. My nightly routine was both spraying peroxide in my hair and applying Ambi to my face. Surely, something would get lighter.

The artist Nastassja Swift writes about her own struggles with her complexion:

> At such a young age, I was unaware of the existence of the word "colorism" and its meaning. Nor had I realized that there were other little girls and boys of color who too were taunted for their complexion. I often thought, *what if I were just a little bit lighter?* In 2018 I Googled the definition of the word "concealer." To mask dark spots on the skin. Those were the words that I read, and immediately I felt a bit uncomfortable thinking about what

> it feels like, and has felt like, to think of yourself as a dark spot in need of masking.[3]

Similarly, because of how I had been treated and the subliminal messages I'd received, to me, lightness equated to goodness. Most importantly for a Black girl who felt ostracized, lightness equated to acceptance. Lightness equated to belonging. Even more jarring was one of the messages that came right from Scripture: "God is light and in him there is no darkness at all" (1 John 1:5).

In church and from my family's teaching, I learned that human beings are created in the image of God. We memorized Genesis 1:27: "So God created humans in his image, in the image of God he created them; male and female he created them." There are different theological interpretations of "image of God." At times "image of God" felt metaphorical, and other times I interpreted it as meaning that I bore a physical resemblance to God. At the same time, based on Psalm 139:14, I was also often reminded (as were other women in the church) that I was fearfully and wonderfully made. I struggled with this because I did not feel fearfully and wonderfully made. Oftentimes, I felt insecure and hated my dark skin and kinky hair. On the one hand, I was told that I was the image of our divine Creator, and on the other hand, I was diminished by society's arbitrary standards for me. Because of this contradiction, I carried a deep-rooted self-hatred that manifested itself in harmful ways, like attempting to lighten my skin and hair. In her master's thesis, "Black Hair and the *Imago Dei*: An Embodiment for God's Vision of Wholeness,"

Keturah Colgate asks, "If I am created in the likeness and image of God, why have I had to physically and chemically alter my God-given features to be and feel accepted in society?"[4]

This was the tension I felt in my Black girlhood.

"What Do You Mean Jesus Looks Like You?"

Star, age fourteen, believes that she is made in the image of God but also wonders if she is truly convinced of that. If she were, then "I wouldn't take in as much as I take in, in regard to my weight or my skin or my acne," she says. "There are all these layers to being a woman and being Black. There is a disconnect as to which message I believe more often. I tend to believe the negative ones, and the image of God should speak so much more power over me."

Therein lies the conflict: Black girls internalize the message that they are created in the image of God, but the world perceives them as less than. I first wrote about my thoughts around Black girlhood and the image of God in *Parable of the Brown Girl*: "Black girls are made in the image of God. While this shouldn't be a revolutionary statement, it is because of how rarely people acknowledge this fact. Black girls hear far more messages about how their aesthetic falls short of traditional beauty standards than they hear about how they embody God's image."[5]

These facts ring true across generations and are why Black girls have to grapple with reconciling their identity with the *imago Dei*. A theological term rooted in Genesis

1:27, *imago Dei* means that human beings are created in the image and likeness of God. Many Black girls, however, have not heard of this theological term.

"What comes to mind when you hear *imago Dei*?" I asked thirteen-year-old Deidre.

"I've . . . never heard that phrase ever," she said.

"Okay, what about you being made in the image of God?"

"I've definitely heard that," Deidre responded.

Though there are different interpretations of the term, hearing it as a Black girl evokes a meaning of physical resemblance. The phrase says not "personality of God" but "image," which naturally draws a young mind to actual physical representation. Sixteen-year-old Imani shared with me that she believed she was literally made in God's image until one day she was told that she was not.

"This one girl, let's call her Macy. Super religious girl. This one time, in fifth grade, I was talking to her about God. I remember saying to her, 'I love that he looks like me too,' and she said, 'What? Jesus is White.' Imagine a fifth-grade Black girl being told that Jesus was White for the first time. I got into a full-blown argument with this girl. That really made me question, What does God actually look like? I felt like I had been lied to, like my church had been lying to me and I didn't know the real God."

She says that she went to church that Sunday, but she didn't pay attention. She no longer believed what they were saying because she had been told that Jesus didn't look like her. It was important that Jesus represented her.

This is how she understood the *imago Dei*. Unfortunately, this is when she slowly began to inch back from her faith.

Some may wonder, what's the big deal? But this was a big deal because Imani imagined her Blackness as a point of connection to God. Without that affirmation, she was lost. Pastor Kevin Young once tweeted, "Imagine how America would be different if every generation had grown up with only brown-eyed, dark-skinned images of Jesus and the disciples. Imagine how diversity would be embraced in America if the explorers and founders had never seen a blue-eyed, white-skinned image of Christ."[6] Likewise, Christena Cleveland reflects on her upbringing and seeing images of a White God in church and how these images were a catalyst for the work she does:

> And so that's a big part of my work, is healing from the way that I was raised. I was raised in a Black family; I'm African American, my parents are African American. But even in a lot of these Black church spaces, and then also some white church spaces that we were also involved in, the image of God was often this white man, either explicitly or implicitly. Sometimes there was the picture up on the stage or near the pulpit, but sometimes it had more to do with the doctrines of patriarchy and white supremacy, patriarchy's BFF. . . . And so, yeah, I grew up in that! Little '80s girl, and started awakening in my early thirties about 10 years ago.[7]

By contrast, Yolanda Pierce never saw a picture of White Jesus in her grandmother's house. She'd seen glimpses of

White Jesus in her friends' houses or even in some Black churches, but she writes, "The Jesus I remember, whose picture was hanging on the wall alongside those of Martin Luther King Jr. and Malcolm X, was a Black man."[8] Pierce says that her grandparents' resistance to connecting Whiteness to divinity was a blessing. "I was an adult before I understood the gift my grandparents had given me: an image of God-in-flesh who looked like me, had hair like me, and had brown skin like mine."[9]

> *At my church, whenever they would lay hands on people they would say to us, "You're made in the image of God," but outside of church people would be telling you to change yourself, so there was a contradiction.—Serena, 14*

Black girls want to be fully accepted and embraced as a part of God's creation. They want to be fully accepted and embraced as the *imago Dei*, and they should be. Otherwise, they are rendered invisible. It is not enough just to say that they are the *imago Dei*; it must be demonstrated. This means that they need to see positive representations of themselves in all aspects of life and spiritual community. They need to see themselves in the woman at the well, a marginalized woman whom Jesus saw and encountered with dignity and respect. They need to see themselves in Mary, the mother of Jesus. They need to see themselves in the disciples, whom Jesus chose to help lead his church. They need to see themselves in the pages and on the walls and in the sermons. When Black girls see representations of their Black skin and hair, they see themselves in God. When this happens, they see themselves as an intentional part of God's creation and can embody a confidence in how they move about in the world.

My friend Alicia, who is in her early forties, went to a Black Christian elementary school. Her teachers made deep connections between Scripture and African heritage. "In my fourth-grade class, I remember distinctly where I would sit," she says. "On the wall was a poster of Jesus, and Jesus had locks. Jesus was a Black man. This was the only representation I'd ever seen of Jesus. I could never identify with people talking about White Jesus, because a lot of my upbringing, Black Jesus was the standard." This was an environment where she says she felt psychologically safe and had a deep sense of pride. It was only when she left this Black school that she began to have a crisis of identity. As an adult, she has spent a great deal of time reflecting on this change. "I always wonder what would have happened if I had stayed at that school. How differently would I see the world or myself?" This is an important question: How differently would Black girls see the world or themselves had they lived in a world where they were represented and treated as the *imago Dei*?

My friend Lisa is raising a biracial daughter. One day her four-year-old daughter said to her, "Mommy, I don't want to be brown." This devastated Lisa, as she wondered what she had done to contribute to this moment. Among other things, Lisa had always intentionally exposed her daughter to entertainment with Black characters and read her books with Black children and bought her Black dolls. Lisa, a pastor, understood that it was important to nurture her daughter's identity as an image bearer of God and a Black girl. Yet Lisa recognized that as much as she tried to do this, she would still have to contend with the countering messages her daughter might receive from the world. "So many messages are sent, not with words, or doctrine, or Scripture, or sermons," she shared with me. "So much of the message of the *imago Dei* is sent with action and incarnation."

When I was very young, my mother was adamant about me having only Black dolls. She noticed that I started expressing a dislike for my dark skin in minor comments that I would make from time to time, and my mom was determined to get out ahead of it. My room was full of Black Barbies and other Black dolls of a wide variety of complexions. Their hair was usually in barrettes or other styles that I was familiar with. One day I visited my friend Taysia's house and saw her room full of White dolls. I was jealous and confused as to why my mom did not allow me to have White dolls too.

My mother, however, understood the connection I would make to my dolls and was determined to make sure I had adequate Black representation around me. My mother told me later that this was important because "I wanted you to have dolls that looked like you. White parents got their daughters dolls that looked like them." Representation is all about the *imago Dei*. How Black girls see themselves represented visually, symbolically, and culturally will have significant implications on how they navigate the world. I believe that it is important how Black girls see themselves represented and that God is deeply concerned with how a lack of representation excludes them as an important part of God's creation. In *Parable of the Brown Girl*, I write that "we are all created by God in God's likeness. The false notion that only one particular type of person reflects God's image causes irreparable damage to Black girls."[10]

It amazes me that so many mothers hear their Black daughters express dislike for their brown skin. One mother says that her daughter, who once was confident in her Blackness, as she was taught, started drawing herself as White with blue eyes after a year in kindergarten. "I don't like my skin color," she told her mother. "I want my skin lighter." One mother said her young daughter burst into tears upon realizing that she wouldn't be able to change her skin.

There has, however, been an evolution of representation in the past thirty years, with more Black and Brown faces in literature, television, politics, and other visible areas of society. This has allowed Black girls to see positive images of themselves, which ultimately contributes to a healthy and positive self-image. This, alongside purposefully teaching love of their Blackness, means that many mothers of Black daughters have not had to experience the blow of having their little girls display an aversion to their skin. While not explicitly theological, this is the message of the *imago Dei*. The *imago Dei* provides us with a theology that values Black girls as part of the divine creation: in their physical nature and character.

I've had a lot of bad self-talk. Teenage girls, we're going to hear things that don't affirm us. I believe in church that I'm in the image of God, but I also, unfortunately, believe what I hear.—Angela, 16

In the midst of their personal struggles with identity and the contradictory and negative messages surrounding their image, Black girls are expected to be resilient. They are expected to bounce back from this adversity and to somehow manage to cope. And while I believe Black girls are resilient, they often struggle to deal with these constant stressors. Many Black girls feel they are not at a place where they can counter these messages on a personal level.

I remember one day I had a really bad day at the White school I attended. I was in middle school. I can't remember what happened exactly, but it was always a mix of microaggressions or just the psychological frustration of being one of the few Black girls in the whole school of a couple hundred students. I came home from school and just laid on the couch. My mom asked me what was wrong, and I just said, "Nothing."—Christina, 41

Black girls don't necessarily have the coping strategies, resources, or emotional maturity to manage the psychological trauma of oppressive messaging or the feelings of being invisible and unheard. At the same time, at their young ages, they should not be expected to. The message of the *imago Dei* should help to counter the pervasive negativity that Black girls are often confronted with. The truth that Black girls are the *imago Dei* should set them free from the lies that society wants them to believe about their identity.

> *Sometimes when I'm struggling, I look at Scripture, and what gets me through is that God is always going to be with me and I know God created me for a reason. That's what gets me through things. There is always a bigger picture.—Kelsey, 14*

Regardless of how they are treated, Black girls are some of the most inclusive human beings in society. It is as though they are born with an understanding of the *imago Dei*. The girls I spoke with often expressed that they want their friends and classmates to feel as though they belong, no matter their race, culture, gender, sexual orientation, or disability. They try to see everyone as having worth and dignity and as fellow image bearers of God.

> *I treat everyone how I want to be treated.—Yara, 17*
>
> *God's point in making us in his image was to make everyone different so maybe we can find our similarities.—Naima, 17*
>
> *It is a sin to allow anybody to diminish the* imago Dei *inside of you.—Carli, 15*

God Sees Me as Beautiful

Awareness of the *imago Dei* is important because of what it tells us about the sacredness of human life. It is a message that is important for Black girls to hear about themselves because it suggests that the divine is not distant but present in them and fosters a sense of interconnectedness and divine purpose. But how effective can the message of the *imago Dei* be in a world infused with so much negativity surrounding Black girls? There are times when I wonder who I would have been had I been born into a world that both celebrated my Black skin and fully honored me as an image bearer of God. Instead, I spent all my girlhood and part of my adulthood vacillating between feelings of shame in some moments and feelings of worthiness in others. I didn't know which message about myself to believe: image of God or image of ugliness?

In an op-ed article in the *Harvard Crimson*, Ebony Smith once wrote, "To be a Black girl in America is to trust that you're beautiful when the world covers the mirrors."[11] I was blessed because I grew up around powerful Black women in my family and Black women leaders in the church who uncovered the mirrors for me. They were my examples. At age fifteen, I wrote a poem that I titled "God Sees Me."

> God sees me as a beautiful child of life.
> God sees me as a unique soul.
> God sees me as a powerful and purposeful person.
> God sees me as an intelligent person.
> God sees me as love in motion.
> God sees me as a child of his.
> So whatever you see doesn't matter, 'cause I care
> how God sees me.

Regardless of how I struggled, in my heart I always knew that I was one of the wonders of God's creation, and I fought to affirm myself despite it all.

Woman*ish* Theodicy

How Black Girls Question Evil and Suffering

Associated Press. May 26, 1998.

A man killed his wife and teen-age daughter with a shotgun early yesterday and then killed himself, the police said.

The police were called to the home of the man, Willie Jordan, at 2:05 AM yesterday by a neighbor who said that Mr. Jordan had come to his house and told him that he had just killed his wife and daughter, the authorities said. Mr. Jordan also said he was going to kill himself, then returned home, the police said. About five minutes later, two officers from Franklin Township arrived at the home and heard what they said sounded like a gunshot.

Police officers from a weapons and tactics team entered the house hours later after telephone calls to the house were unanswered. They found the bodies of Mr. Jordan, 47, his wife,

Margie, 48, and their daughter Norelle, 16, in separate rooms. Mr. Jordan's 22-month-old grandson was found unhurt near Mr. Jordan's body, said the Somerset County Prosecutor, Wayne J. Forrest.[1]

~

Norelle and I met in church when we were just kids. That's where I met most of my close friends. Her mother was an active member, and her father would come to services periodically. Norelle had an older sister named Cynthia who was friends with my older brother. She dressed very cool and dainty, had lighter skin and big green eyes, and sang soprano in our youth choir, Voices of Inspiration. Norelle was the opposite of her sister; back then we would call a girl like her a "tomboy." She had chocolate skin like mine and big brown eyes, and she always wore her hair partially back with her bangs out. Norelle didn't sing in any choirs or participate on youth Sundays. She was more aloof, the kind of person who'd walk up to the guys playing basketball in the park and say to them, "We got next."

That is exactly how we bonded: over basketball. As a matter of fact, a few girls at the church were talented athletes. Deaconess Stevenson decided to get all of us together to form a church basketball team. I was elated by the idea. Outside of church barbeques or block parties, I'd never had the chance to play with Norelle because we went to different schools. Deaconess Stevenson worked out a schedule for us to play against teams from other churches, and we practiced sometimes before church Bible studies or other times when church activities were in session. We weren't a very good team, but I loved playing with my friends and with Norelle.

Before long, though, Norelle and I were off to separate high schools. I still saw her in church from time to time and heard about her being a starter on the Franklin High School girls' basketball team. I was so proud. I was a starter on St. Peter's High School girls' basketball team, but even though we were just a township away, we didn't play each other. One day my coach decided that he wanted to put an AAU (Amateur Athletic Union) basketball team together, and he wanted to call it the Central Jersey Jammers. I called Norelle almost immediately and asked if she would consider joining. She was excited to join, and we recruited another point guard from the area named Wakedra. On the first day of practice, I was elated because I was on a team with some of my high school teammates and two of the most respected players in the area. As much as we thought we would be unstoppable, though, we weren't very good. Most of us played the same position and did not understand how to be a team. Still, like with the church team, I enjoyed playing with my friends and with Norelle.

Memorial Day weekend, 1998, the Central Jersey Jammers were scheduled to play a basketball tournament in Connecticut. I was looking forward to traveling with my team during the holiday weekend. With my bags packed and ready to go, I received word that the tournament was canceled. I was disappointed because this was going to be our first overnight trip as a team. Nevertheless, staying home from school was just as appealing of an option because it meant I got to sleep in. My basement bedroom was perfect for a sixteen-year-old. I had just enough space between me and the rest of the house to feel a sense of independence.

I was so happy to have the day off that my deep, peaceful sleep caused me to miss my phone ringing the first few times. When it rang again, I picked it up and with a raspy voice said, "Hello?"

"Khristi, did you hear? Norelle's dad went crazy and killed her, her mom, and himself and left the baby on the porch!"

I tried to comprehend what was just said to me. "Wait . . . what?" I asked.

"Norelle's dad went crazy and killed her, her mom, and himself and left the baby on the porch!"

A long, awkward pause ensued when my friend realized that this news was more than just gossip.

"Oh. I'm sorry. Y'all were close."

"I'll call you back," I told her.

I hung up the phone and sat on the side of my bed. All I heard in the background was the sound of rain hitting the grass. I looked up and saw how gloomy it was outside through the one compact basement window in the upper corner of my room. I am not sure how long I sat just staring up and out that window. Even though I felt weak in my knees, I finally gathered the strength to walk upstairs. The house was unusually quiet. I opened the basement door and walked into the kitchen to see my mother and aunt turn to look at me.

"Khristi . . ." my mother said.

I stopped her.

"I know," I responded.

I left the kitchen and walked into the living room. As I sat on the couch, the tears began to flow. My mom came into the room and asked if I wanted to talk. I didn't. I just wanted to be alone.

I simply could not comprehend what was happening. Why? How? She was only sixteen. I wondered where Norelle was in the house when her dad killed her. The article, which we read in the paper the next day, said that it was 2:05 a.m. when Mr. Jordan went to tell his neighbor. Did that mean he killed her around midnight? Was she asleep? Maybe she was up late watching television since she didn't have to go to school the next day. If she was awake, did she hear him kill her mother first and try to get up to fight him? I pictured Cynthia coming home from a long evening of work to the nightmare of having her family taken from her in an instant. I wondered why Mr. Jordan spared the baby's life. I hated that I had to grapple with these questions as a sixteen-year-old. (It now feels selfish to say that, knowing that so many young people today, including Black girls just like I was, must grapple with the realities of violence almost daily.) I had many questions. I had so many thoughts. I thought that she would still be alive if we had gone to that tournament. I needed someone to blame. I was angry at whoever had canceled the tournament because had we been away, my friend would not have died.

And finally, where was God? Why would God allow this to happen? Those were the thoughts that went through my mind as I sat on the couch in my living room that morning and in the days to come. I wrestled with the theological question, Why would a good God allow such a bad thing to happen? I grappled with theodicy. Theodicy attempts to explain evil alongside the reality of an all-knowing and all-powerful God. In his book *Faith Seeking Understanding*, theologian Daniel Migliore says, "The question of theodicy is often stated in the form: If God is both perfectly good and all-powerful, why does evil exist?"[2] Theodicy seeks to address the contradiction between the existence of a loving and omnipotent God and the existence of evil and suffering in the world. Suffering in the lives of Black people in America has always been unique because the Black experience in America began with slavery and forced labor. To this day, Black Americans continue to be impacted by the trauma of that past in addition to the effects of structural racism. Theodicy in the Black experience explores liberation from that suffering and considers the purpose of suffering and the nature of an all-powerful God. I'd known all my life that the world is full of evil, but I'd never been confronted with a quandary like this—why the all-powerful and all-knowing God I served would not stop *this* evil that took my friend and her family away so swiftly and violently.

The day I returned to school was awkward and uncomfortable. Everyone had heard what had happened, but no one knew what to say to me or how to interact with me. They too were just teenagers who did not necessarily have the emotional intelligence to respond to such a painful situation. Like me, they did not understand what it meant to have their world tragically interrupted. I went to find my friends Andre and Monique. I knew them as my laughing friends because we would laugh all day every day. Yet today was it appropriate to laugh? Monique just looked at me with a straight face, and Andre acknowledged the moment by saying, "I heard what happened. That sucks." Yes, it did suck. Then we went on about our school day as normally as we knew how.

On the way home from school, the song "The Arms of the One Who Loves You" by Xscape came on the radio station. The song had just come out a few months prior and was on the Billboard Hot 100 and Hot R&B/Hip-Hop Songs chart. The song is about a person in love with someone who they realize they must let go in order for the person to be happy. Something about the lyrics stood out to me on the car ride. When I got home, I went straight downstairs to my room. I did not want to talk about it because I did not want my parents acting weird around me, though they had every reason to be concerned. I went to my boom box and put in the Xscape album that had the song I'd heard on the radio. The singer says that she knows the person she loves is going and she can't make them stay, but she lets them know that she loves them anyway. She tells them that wherever the road takes them, they should know that they can run back to her arms because she will be there waiting. "When rain has found your heart never fear, I'm never far. You just run to the arms of the one who loves you,"[3] she sings.

The song isn't about death or grief, but the lyrics hit me hard. The tears began to flow again, and I thought of the song as a letter from me to my friend Norelle. I listened to the song on repeat for hours, and eventually I made my way to my bed to lie down. As the tears streamed down my face, I drifted off to sleep in my school uniform, thinking good thoughts of my friend and wondering if she knew how much I loved her.

The day of the funeral I insisted on going to school for the first half of the day. The funeral wouldn't begin until early in the afternoon, and I wanted to go with my teammates. My parents were very understanding that I wouldn't be going with them. They were both church leaders, so they would be at the church early anyway. I wore my funeral outfit to school. My blouse was lime green, and I wore black pants and low heels. For someone who did not want to draw any attention to her grief, I sure chose a color that would make me stand out among the plaid Catholic school uniforms. When it was time for the van to pick us up to go to the funeral, Andre and Monique sat with me on the steps in front of the school gym. I have no recollection of what we talked about, but I remember that their presence was my comfort.

My teammates and I all piled into the van to head over to the church. It couldn't have been more than a ten-minute ride, but it felt like an hour. On the ride over, gospel songs played on the radio. Perhaps the driver was playing gospel as a way of preparing our spirits for what we were about to experience. I remember hearing Fred Hammond's song "No Way, No Way (You Won't Lose)." The song is about a man who wakes up one morning thinking that it will be a normal day, only to get a call and have his world cave in.

How could those lyrics be so spot-on? That was exactly what happened to me the morning I found out Norelle had been killed. As the song continues, Hammond sings, "I hear You, Lord (I hear You, Lord), reassuring me again, again. You have shown You're in control of everything."[4]

I felt like God was telling me that he was in control. I felt comforted—but also confused. If God was in control, then how and why was any of this happening? I found it interesting that the soundtrack to this week of grief and tragedy was an R&B song followed by a gospel song, neither of which had anything to do with the other. The gospel music I listened to and the sermons I heard preached often spoke of God being in control of everything. In theology, this is often referred to as providence. There is "the quality in divinity on which humankind bases the belief in a benevolent intervention in human affairs and the affairs of the world."[5] I understood providence to mean that God governs the world with care, protection, love, and wisdom. Yet, providence was difficult to process because of the reality of evil and suffering. I wanted to believe that God had complete control, but if that were the case, it made no sense why God would allow this evil to happen to Norelle. The stages of grief were upon me as I went from denial and confusion to anger. I felt that I had nowhere to direct my anger but toward God. *Why would God do this?* I kept thinking to myself. This was my introduction to "protest theodicy," which Migliore describes as a theodicy that questions the total goodness of God. He writes, "This is a theodicy with no easy answers but with the honesty to raise what earlier believers would have considered blasphemous questions and with a determination to be faithful to God even when it appears that God has ceased to be faithful."[6]

When we arrived, the parking lot was packed. We were let out at the front of the church, and the first person I saw in the lobby was my mother. She was there watching and waiting for me, knowing that I would be with my teammates but being her usual supportive presence. The service hadn't started, and we came right before the viewing was to end. I looked around and saw that the pews were filled with many people I did not recognize. I turned my attention to the front of the sanctuary, where all three bodies were in caskets at the altar. I had no idea that all three bodies would be there. I thought I was attending just the funeral for Norelle.

I walked with my teammates down to the front, where I paused and looked at Mrs. Jordan's peaceful body as she lay in her casket. I proceeded to walk toward Norelle, who was in the center. She wore her basketball jersey. It was white, gold, and blue and said Franklin High School, 23. Like most basketball players, she looked up to Michael Jordan and wore his number throughout her basketball career. There was my homegirl looking beautiful with her hair in her standard bang. It was quite a disconcerting sight for a sixteen-year-old to witness in a crowded room full of onlookers just days after a tragedy that I had yet to process or wrap my mind around. Norelle's father was in the third casket on the other side of the altar. I walked past without acknowledging the body. *How dare they have him in the same funeral? How dare they have a funeral for him at all?*

As I angrily contemplated what kind of message Norelle's family was trying to send by having him there, I looked up and noticed Cynthia, tears streaming from eyes that were red with grief. In that moment, I realized they were her family, all three of them. How difficult it must have been losing all of them at the hands of her own father, whom she loved. It must have been a difficult decision for her to have his body present as well.

My teammates and I had a special reserved section. After we viewed the bodies, we walked to that area and took our seats. During the service, I thought about the last conversation I had with Norelle. Basketball practice had ended, and both of us were waiting in the parking lot for our rides. It had been a late practice, so it was dark outside. We talked about the upcoming tournament in Connecticut, and we talked strategy a bit. After that I said, "Girl, I haven't seen you in church in a while. What's up?"

Norelle responded, "I don't believe in God or anything like that anymore. I believe in the stars and the birds and stuff."

"Oh," I said hesitantly. "Okay, cool."

Her mother arrived to pick her up, and we said we'd see each other at the tournament. The tournament was canceled, and that was the last time I saw Norelle alive.

A rush of panic overcame me in the sanctuary. *Oh my God! I told Norelle that it was okay that she didn't believe in God! Was Norelle in hell because of me? Is there a hell?* I felt like I had been a bad witness to the gospel in such a crucial moment. I had grown up in church and been to services and listened to sermons and sung in choirs and participated in ministries, yet I had missed this one opportunity to share the faith I said I believed in with my friend. A wave of guilt overcame me and stayed with me for the remainder of the service, so much so that the program felt more like background noise to my thoughts. I hung my head in shame, feeling as though I had let Norelle down and I had let God down.

These thoughts would carry over into the summer of 1998 and subsequently into my senior year in high school. I had the typical fun-filled senior year, but Norelle was always in the back of my mind; I was still processing my feelings of grief and guilt. Picking up a basketball, something I once loved, was overshadowed by grief and guilt. When basketball season began, I was only a shadow of the player I once was. The desire to play basketball in college waned as the months went on, and I was at a crossroads. My constant thought was that "life's short," a phrase brought on by the untimely death of my friend.

"Trouble Don't Last Always"[7]

I wrote the following poem one night when I was thirteen years old, three years before Norelle died.

> Why is everyone laughing?
> How could they have a good time knowing there's
> another soul out there desperate and crying?
> When there's killing and dying, no one is trying.
> No one goes out of their way when someone is
> crying.

Not everyone has a smile if you open your eyes
and see.
Not everyone is sleeping peaceful at night
Or dreaming without a fright.
Others tremble in their sleep,
It's their lives they're trying to keep.

I am not sure what circumstances surrounded its writing, but it is clear that when I was a young teenager, pain was a puzzle that I explored even in my limited understanding. Evil and suffering are an inescapable part of human existence. The problem of evil is that there are evils of malicious intent and there are circumstantial or natural evils that are beyond our control. The other problem of evil, for theists, is that God—omniscient, omnipotent, and omnipresent—both exists and allows evil to exist: "The classic theological question of evil centers around the problem of reconciling the historical presence of evil and the belief that God is the all-good, all-powerful Creator of the universe. How could an all-good God be the source of evil? How could an all-good God permit evil? Why doesn't an all-powerful God prevent or eliminate evil?"[8]

Black girls definitely experience the evil and suffering of the human condition. They experience loss, pain, and hurt like any other human being. There is evil in the possibility of mass shootings, pandemics, cruelty, and illness. But for Black girls, there are also painful experiences that have to do with race. There is evil that comes from oppression, discrimination, and abuse. Black girls have inherited the evil and suffering of their ancestral line from chattel slavery and institutionalized racism. They have inherited sexism and misogyny. They experience suffering that happens due to circumstances and suffering owing to their very existence. Theodicy asks, "If God is a good God, then why does evil exist?" and for the Black girl, theodicy asks, "If God is a good God, then why does evil occur simply because I exist?" Questions arise from theodicy and attempts are made to answer them, but the only sure fact is that these questions will never be answered with any certainty. Nevertheless, we still ask.

When Norelle died, I had questions about why this happened to her, but she was also the victim of domestic violence, and I became starkly aware of the deafening silence surrounding this issue that occurred after her death. Black women and girls experience domestic violence at significantly higher rates than White women, and while this was the first time I experienced it firsthand, it would not be the last time I would observe the injustice of Black girls suffering the world's evils.

Sixteen-year-old Nyasia shared with me that she was raised by her mother alone, with little support from extended family, and had never met her father. Her mother struggled with addiction after a routine surgery left her in more pain than she could bear. Her mother lost her job, and eventually they lost their home and had to move to live with her grandmother. As time went on, Nyasia's mother became addicted to other drugs, which evolved into a pattern of emotional abuse and neglect of Nyasia. "There was a lot of name-calling," Nyasia said. "I had to take care of my mother so much that I missed a lot of school. It went from being a lot to this is my every day."

Nyasia was failing all her classes. Her teachers blamed her poor study habits and absence from school, yet no one asked her why she missed school or what was happening in her life that was causing her to struggle. This disregard by teachers and/or administrators is not an uncommon experience for Black girls. Shawn Arango Ricks writes, "In order to work towards connecting and creating environments in which Black girls can thrive, educational administrators, teachers and families need to increase their awareness of the unique issues Black girls face. This must be done at both institutional and individual levels."[9] Nyasia's unfortunate circumstances caused her to fall through the cracks both in her home life and at school. Like with other Black girls, no one noticed her pain because they were too focused on her failures. In sharing her story with me, she talked about how she wrestled with her circumstances: "I asked my grandmother, Why do I have to have this life? Why couldn't I live like some of my friends who are happy, and their parents are together, and they live with like a white picket fence? One day when I get a chance to talk to God, I'm going to ask him."

Nyasia's mother tried to get clean when Nyasia turned fourteen—the year they went to live with her grandmother. She stayed sober for a short while but then started using drugs again. When this happened, Nyasia knew that she needed to prepare herself for the worst. "I knew I would wake up one morning and my mother would be dead, and I would be left to fend for myself. I knew I would be on my own." One evening after Nyasia had just turned fifteen, her grandmother came into her room crying to tell her that her mother had died from an overdose. Nyasia had to process simultaneously the death of her mother, the evil of drug addiction, and the painful reality that she was a young Black girl now alone in this world. "I see it as I was given this type of life because maybe God knew that I could deal with it," she told me. "I grew from this. I was angry that I even had to deal with it at all. There have been times I would say I regret this life. But it made me into the person I am today. Don't get me wrong, I'm still angry. But I don't blame myself or God."

Like Nyasia, many Black girls take a redemptive approach in response to evil and suffering. While evil may not be overcome, growth, strength, and transformation can emerge from it. When Nyasia says that her difficult life made her into the person she is today, she suggests that her suffering was a part of her process of becoming.[10] She embraces her discomfort and believes that her experiences are a part of her development as a human being. Giving meaning to the pain is a primary way that Black girls choose to survive in this evil world.

Sometimes you have to go through things to get stronger.
—Kayla, 13

The evils may come, but Black girls become stronger, more resilient, and wiser as a result. This is womanish resistance: not being overcome by evil but overcoming evil with good (see Rom. 12:21). In this instance, the good is in the imperfect process of becoming. The process of becoming addresses the fundamental question of how we as individuals evolve, transform, and develop over time. Black girls approach difficult situations as an opportunity to grow. Each challenge they overcome equips them with valuable life skills and resilience.

Black girls also practice womanish resistance when they choose gratitude as a response to evil and suffering. This by no means suggests that Black girls should be grateful for their misfortunes. Instead, they sometimes choose gratitude as a means of survival.

> *Life is hard, so I love harder. Maybe too hard at times. I take family time more seriously. I take my time with friends more seriously. I take the time to appreciate the small things.*
> *—Jasmine, 18*

Sometimes evil and suffering can blind us to the good that surrounds us. By choosing gratitude, Black girls find light in the midst of the darkness. They do not have to be grateful, nor are they always grateful, but there are moments when they turn their focus to the good that is present. A Black girl's faith is strengthened as she acknowledges her lack of control and turns to the grace she has been given.

> *These things make me reevaluate why I am here. If bad things can happen to the person next to me, what makes me so special? What makes my family so special? That's tough to think about. I am grateful for what we have, and I*

promised myself that I would do things that I want to do in the moments.—Brooke, 16

I am incredibly grateful for the people I have around me right now. Sometimes I lay in bed at night scared to lose it. Thoughts that you shouldn't be thinking at night, but I do. I am almost paralyzed by "What's going to happen?" But then I remind myself that I'm good. I'm here. I try to ground myself.—Alana, 14

Despite Black girls' resilience in the face of evil and suffering, tragedies can also play a role in them losing their faith. At first they believe in God, who is supposed to be loving and omnipotent, but then they struggle to reconcile this belief with the existence of suffering and tragedy, especially if they experience it personally. After being sexually assaulted, one young woman shared, "If God is real and he's supposed to help save me and be good, then why would he let stuff like that happen to me? It wasn't just the grooming; it was even my self-confidence being taken down. I prayed. I asked God to protect me. Why didn't he protect me when I needed him to protect me? That's when I became agnostic. That really tested my faith." In the most extreme cases, evil and suffering can end a Black girl's faith.

Others may not lose their faith but simply continue to ask questions. Meredith has polycystic ovary syndrome (PCOS), and she wonders how to deal with the existence of evil. She knows God is good but cannot comprehend suffering. "If God really created us and loves us, then why does cancer exist?" she questions. "I just don't get sickness and diabetes. If we were made in God's image, why do I have PCOS at fifteen years old?" Black girls are not afraid to ask the difficult questions and the foundational question of theodicy: "Why?" Generally, people fear questioning God, but for Black girls, asking is a process of self-reflection and exploration. Some seek to reconcile their faith with their questions, even though they may not get answers.

If God didn't create evil, then why is evil here? Obviously, we don't understand the reason and God does, but sometimes it makes me really confused. Like what was the point of having Satan? Didn't God create him? So did God create evil? That's something I tussle with.—Jocelyn, 18

If the tree of good and evil was there and put there by God, if everything started with God and everything is how it is because of the series of events, did God eventually do it this way so that the outcome would be this? I want to say God didn't intend this. If he didn't, then why not intervene?—Lili, 13

Part of Black girls' resilience is to push forward in spite of evil. The womanist tradition calls us to do more than just respond to evil and suffering. Womanism teaches us that God calls us to joy. Joy can coexist with suffering, offering hope and strength in the face of adversity. As they process evil and suffering, Black girls also choose joy. They choose to create change and meaning for themselves out of life's difficulties. One woman reflected on an unnamed tragedy that occurred in her community when she was a teenager: "I did not have time to process trauma. It was more like okay this happened, now let's stand up and fight. We took the suffering and turned it into something meaningful. We had to have a response for it. We never sat with the grief or the death. It was like 'Alright, so what we gonna do?'"

Black girls also respond to evil and suffering with unique perspectives. Some accept that evil and suffering are a part of life. Some believe they have a choice in how they react. One girl said to me, "Instead of putting all the blame on God, what could *we* do to address the reality of suffering and evil?" Others see their faith in a God who is present with them in their suffering as enough to sustain them.

> *I like to think of it as God sent his Son to the world. Like this terrible, terrible world. It's the world that's terrible, and God sent Jesus to save us from its terribleness. And I think that is really really special.—Isa, 17*

Tragedy's Deeper Meaning

"Tell us about a significant challenge or adversity you have faced in your life. Describe the situation, your initial thoughts and emotions, and the steps you took to overcome it. What did you learn from this experience, and how has it shaped your perspective, values, or goals?"

The college essay prompt for my application to Temple University was straightforward, and my response did not require much contemplation. It had been less than six months since I'd experienced one of the worst moments of my life. The challenge was losing Norelle so suddenly and violently. The steps I took to overcome it—I was still in the process of figuring that out. How it shaped my perspective was that I was left with questions that I'd never thought much about before. What was my purpose? Why was she gone and I was still here? My childhood faith was unquestioned, but after Norelle's death, my faith was growing into a new phase. I suppose, in some strange way, the tragedy that occurred gave me a different perspective on life and made me value the people God had placed in my life, like my family and friends. Suffering, tragedy, and grief have a way of pointing us toward the things that have deeper meaning and away from anything unimportant that we give too much attention to. Even when it came time to apply to and choose a college, that is exactly what I had in mind. Where could I go that would be a community where I could grow strong relationships and where I could seek out meaning and purpose?

It has been over thirty years since Norelle was killed, and it astounds me how much I still think about her. That time of my life was so long ago and brief, but it had such an effect on me that I think even the vocational path I chose was influenced by that tragedy. As an adult, I have committed myself to helping youth in their own spiritual journeys and helping them navigate crises of faith. There are easy parts of the faith journey, and there are painful parts. I hate that some Black girls (or any young people) have to work through the hard parts on their own. I am grateful that I was never left alone in the difficult seasons of my spiritual journey. I always had my family and a strong faith community to help guide me through those times. Having to experience suffering is one thing; it's another to process the harsh reality of evil and suffering theologically. I will never understand why Norelle died the way she did, cut off from the possibility of a full life at such a young age. In spite of this, I channeled that experience into creating a life of meaning for myself that honors both the questions and the lessons that arose from that moment in time.

5

Woman*ish* Theology of Prayer

How Black Girls Talk with God

"It's prayer time!"

My great-grandmother Mama Rosella would stand outside the front door of the house and shout these words to my aunts and uncle each night when they were kids.

"We would be outside playing," my mother recalls, "but we knew we had to be home at six o'clock to pray no matter where we were. Around five minutes to six, if we were not on our way back, Mama would stand out on the porch and scream, 'Antoinette! Greg! Kids, it's prayer time!' All our friends knew that we had to stop, go home, and pray. Sometimes they would come with us. And you better come or else you wouldn't be out there playing anymore. Or you'd get a whoopin'."

Prayer has been in the DNA of our family for generations. Mama Rosella continued a tradition that was passed down to her of praying three times a day: six o'clock in the morning, twelve noon, and six in the evening. Not only did Mama Rosella commit to praying at these times, but she expected the entire family to pray at these times as well. My mother lived with my great-grandmother; her five siblings, Veda, Greg, Heather, Toxi, and Jane; and my great-uncle Bunk. The eight of them lived on Dexter Street in Rocky Mount, North Carolina, in a small, three-room row house that was called a "shotgun house" because you could shoot a gun straight through it. The house consisted of a front room/living room, a middle room, which was the only bedroom, and a kitchen. They did not have much, but they had each other. And they had the traditions that had been passed down through our family, prayer being a significant one.

Prayer was always done as a family except during the school year, when the children were at school (but even then, they were expected to pray individually). When they prayed as a family, Mama Rosella would lead the prayer. My mom shared with me her memories of prayer as a little girl growing up on Dexter Street:

> In the evening we would not just pray. We would also sing a song. I don't remember if we said the Lord's Prayer or another prayer. When we were finished, we would go back outside to play. It was the discipline. It taught us the value of prayer. Prayer was a part of our life and our lifestyle.

There were also certain times of the year when my family would have what they referred to as "Holy Convocation," a weeklong assembly where they would gather at

> four a.m. next door at the home of my great-aunt, who was referred to as "Aunt Sister," and her husband, Elder Piccot. There they would sing songs and pray together as a family. We were pretty much our own church. We would assume various postures for prayer each morning. Sometimes we would pray sitting up or lying down. There were seven different postures. I remember being so sleepy. I was as young as six years old. I couldn't wait to go back to sleep!

The consistency of having prayer three times a day continued from when my mother was a child to when she moved to New York when she was fourteen years old to live with my grandmother, Mama Hattie. Even though the siblings moved, the practice and prioritization of prayer never ended. My mom told me, "For us, prayer was what we did. No matter what, you stopped to pray."

As I mentioned in chapter 1, I have vivid memories of watching Mama Hattie spend time with the Lord. This was both her time reading Scripture and her time in prayer. This was a sacred time that was not to be disturbed. I also have memories of Mama Hattie and me kneeling on the side of the bed, and I repeated the Lord's Prayer after her. I did this at home with my own mother as well. To this day, my mother spends time alone in her room, sitting on the side of the bed reading Scripture and praying, just as my grandmother and great-grandmother did.

In her book *In My Grandmother's House*, womanist theologian and scholar Yolanda Pierce writes about the theology she gleaned from her grandmother's wisdom.

The faith that she encountered as a young Black girl came from her grandmother. Her memories of prayer are similar to mine and my mother's: "My grandmother's internal clock rang early, and so she rose early in the morning to pray."[1] As a girl, Pierce would sneak over to hear her talk to Jesus. "She knelt down beside her bed to pray, and she taught me that kneeling was the proper form in which to pray."[2] Pierce was just six years old, forming her own theology of prayer as she observed her grandmother kneeling to pray at the feet of Jesus. "I would listen very quietly, as she completely unburdened herself before Jesus, in the way of two longtime friends, who barely have to finish their sentences to make their thoughts known to each other."[3] Pierce sums up her early theological teachings, writing, "My Christology begins at the foot of my bed with a grandmother teaching me to sing words I have hidden in my heart and to which I return even when prayers sometimes fail."[4]

I can confidently say the same. My Christology began with my grandmothers and my parents. Christology is a branch of theology that explores the nature, person, and work of Jesus Christ. It delves into questions about the identity of Jesus, examining both his divinity and his humanity as well as the relationship between the two. Prayer played a significant role in shaping my Christology, influencing my understanding of and relationship with Jesus. I was taught that prayer is communion with Jesus. Having a "personal relationship with Christ" was shaped by my belief that through prayer we are intimately connected to God through Christ. This is why it was always so important to end every prayer with an emphasized "in Jesus's name, amen!" We were essentially acknowledging that our only access to God was through Jesus in prayer. I distinctly recall as a child that at times someone would end a prayer with just "amen," and I would shudder, wondering if we needed to call the name of Jesus. My theology of prayer was formed by these early teachings and observations.

The sacred tradition of prayer that began generations ago has continued in our family throughout the years. I have vivid memories of us gathering as a family no matter how large or small. Before any of us would travel (or as we called it, "get on the road"), my parents, siblings, and I would hold hands and pray. Over the holidays, more than a dozen of us would travel, and before we set out, we would all hold hands and pray. Aunt Mary, Uncle Greg, or my dad would usually be asked to pray, and they would pray for traveling mercies and special blessings for our family. My dad would always pray that God would keep us "on the highways and the byways," which basically meant on the busy roads and on the small or side roads. We prayed longer prayers as a family before special meals on Thanksgiving, Christmas, and Easter. On Thanksgiving, we would first go around the room and say what we were thankful to God for, and then Aunt Mary, Uncle Greg, or Dad would lead the prayer. Aunt Mary would always start with "Heavenly Father, I want to thank you!" During the prayers, I would often hear other members of the family say, "Yes, Lord," "Yes, Father," and "Thank you, Jesus." I remember as a little girl that I would open my eyes to see what was happening during the prayer. Oftentimes, my hands would start sweating because the prayers would go so long. I never felt forced to pray. In my young mind, all families prayed like this. Prayer was an extension of our identity, and praying to, thanking, and petitioning God were just as natural as anything else to me.

The Black church has a rich history and a unique approach to prayer that reflect our cultural and spiritual heritage. The tradition of prayer began during the institution of slavery. Before the creation of the Black church, our ancestors would sneak away to pray, sing, and dance, despite the threat of violence and death, because they knew that God was important to their survival. Melva Wilson Costen writes that the tradition of Black prayer "speaks more to the African understanding of God than it does to the American form of Christianity to which the slaves were introduced."[5] Since the time of slavery, Black people have continued the tradition of prayer even in the face of religious and personal persecution. For our community, prayer is connected not just to a church building but to our collective experience as a people. Our prayers have been forged in the face of adversity. For generations, prayer in the Black church has been rooted in spirituality, community, and cultural expression. It is a fundamental and integral aspect of our religious experience.

Prayer was an important spiritual practice that was a part of my church community. Our church prayed for everything. The deacons would pray before the start of the service. They'd lead the worshipers in singing hymns and pray for different members of the congregation. Then the worship service was built around prayer and the sermon, which we referred to as "the word of God." We started services with music, which was followed by the invocation prayer, during which we called on God to be with us during and to bless the service. In the middle of the service, the pastor or another minister would come to the altar and simply say, "It's prayer time." The organ would play softly, and the congregation would rise. The minister would instruct us to grab the hands of our neighbors as we went before God in prayer. As a girl, I dreaded this part of the service because it was usually a long prayer, and my hands would get hot and sweaty holding the hands of the people next to me. The congregation felt more emotionally connected to this prayer than any of the others. The prayer offered was always for those who were sick and shut-in, for the pastor and his family, for congregants in need of healing or a blessing, and for the health and strength of us as a church.

For special services, like on Easter or New Year's Eve, the prayers were usually much longer. Our New Year's Eve service was called "Watch Night Service," a celebration that has historical significance for the Black community and typically marks the end of an old year and the beginning of a new year. The service commemorates December 31, 1862, when enslaved African Americans gathered in churches to await the Emancipation Proclamation, which was set to take effect on January 1, 1863. Since then, within many Black churches, the Watch Night Service has become a cultural and spiritual tradition as we transition from the old year to the new year, symbolizing new beginnings. Growing up, I always spent New Year's Eve at church.

There was never any other option for us as a family. I found it strange that my friends would go to parties or have other events that night because I was taught that we were supposed to "pray into the New Year."

At the end of the Watch Night Service, when there were about fifteen minutes left before midnight, we would all stand and hold hands as a congregation, as we did at a normal Sunday service. This time we would pray until after midnight. Pastor Buster Soaries always made sure not to end his prayer before midnight. Those prayers felt endless, but I never complained because it always felt right to me that we would end the year with God and begin the year with God. It felt right that we would spend that time thanking God for how far he had brought us and asking God to be with us in the next year. I was just a little girl, but I understood the significance of those moments.

I was surrounded by prayer in my home and at church, and though I knew the Lord's Prayer and how to say grace, I thought I had just a basic understanding of how to pray. My first time praying out loud in a public space was at the end of a youth choir rehearsal. At the end of every rehearsal, the choir director would call on one of the young people to pray aloud. To me, these prayers were always powerful, and the pianist would often play quietly in the background for dramatic effect while the person was praying. I was so nervous at the end of every rehearsal because I knew the time would come when I would be asked to pray. In my mind, I didn't know *how* to pray. In the Black church, there is the spiritual practice of prayer, which is personal, and then there is praying in public, which feels performative at times. I come from a religious tradition in which demonstration in prayer is considered holy. Anita Phillips says, "Sound is sacred in traditional African worldviews and so we're loud. And I think we were made for it. There's just something about the sound of our voices. We make music with our bodies. We clap our hands. We show God how we feel."[6]

Later in life, I realized that I am more of a contemplative worshiper, but I didn't have the words to articulate that then. My silent, personal prayers were one thing because they were between me and God. Praying out loud in a public setting meant that I couldn't take too many pauses and I had to say the right words and use the right cadence. Sometimes when the end of rehearsal came, I made sure not to make eye contact with the choir director because I did not want us to lock eyes and my name to come out of his mouth. Eventually, the day did come when I was asked to pray. I started off the same way Aunt Mary would in our family prayers: "Heavenly Father, before we say another word, Lord, we just want to thank you." "Thank you!" other voices shouted in echo. That was all the encouragement I needed to keep going. I got through that prayer and was very proud of myself after. My peers and some of the adult volunteers looked at me as though to give their stamp of approval. Perhaps I really was anointed.

As I got older, prayer became more personal, or so I was taught that it was supposed to be. I had always been active in the youth ministry at church. It was called JAM, which stood for "Jesus and Me." The name was indicative of its mission: to bring young people closer to Jesus. All the teaching was geared toward our generation. JAM was cool and relevant. We were taught that our salvation was more than just one moment or event. It was about living a Christian lifestyle and maintaining a personal relationship with Jesus Christ.

The concept of a "personal relationship" with Jesus was the foundation of what I was taught about prayer. You could not have one without the other. Different Christian traditions emphasize the concept to varying degrees, but it is a central aspect of evangelical theology and practice. Though we were Baptist, I always felt our youth ministry was different, and looking back now I realize that we were heavily influenced by 1990s evangelical Christianity. The concept of a personal relationship with Jesus was one that most young people could wrap their minds around. It was relatable. This was how prayer was introduced to me, on a level that I could understand. Our youth leader, Mike Pinnix, used to tell us to just "pull up a chair and talk to God." One day I did.

I came home from school and was upset about something that happened that day. I stared at the empty chair at the desk in my room as I recalled what Mike had told us. I pulled the chair closer to my window. I sat in silence for a few minutes, thinking that it would be weird to start talking to an empty chair. I let out a hesitant, "Hi, God." This was nothing like praying out loud in front of everyone after choir rehearsal. I knew God didn't care much about fancy words or cadence. This was less about saying the right thing and more about speaking from my heart. I proceeded to go through the order in which I was taught to pray. I was taught to thank God before asking for anything, so I went into my thank-you list, thanking God for my parents and my family. I thanked God for my school. I thanked God for my life and breath and my friends. There was a lot to be thankful for. Then I talked to God about my day and asked for his help with a few things, like the issues I was having with my friend and the problems on my basketball team. Talking to God in that empty chair became easier the longer I kept going. It wasn't so bad after all. From that point on, pulling up that empty chair became a regular practice for me.

"I Had a Praying Grandmother"

American singer and songwriter Helen Baylor once shared her testimony about being a seven-year-old Black girl growing up in the church. She recalled her grandmother taking her to church and how she loved going with her and singing songs to the Lord. Her immediate family moved when she was eleven, but her grandmother stayed back. The family stopped going to church after they moved, and Baylor's life was one of many difficulties. She went on to say, "The devil was trying to kill me, but I had a praying grandmother who never turned her back on me."[7]

"I had a praying grandmother and a praying mama" is a phrase I have often heard and have repeated myself. I often wonder, if not for their prayers and how they kept prayer at the forefront of our family, where or who would I be today?

Prayer is one concept that even those who are not active in the faith have a basic understanding of. While Black people do not all ascribe to a particular religious tradition, prayer tends to be understood by Black people regardless of religious belief. Prayer is just as much a part of Black culture as it is a part of religion. Black women and girls have their own unique understanding of prayer and are often taught about prayer by those who came before them—namely, grandmothers or parents.

Martha, a fifty-six-year-old woman, shared how she was exposed to prayer as a young Black girl, a story similar to that of my mother: "I was always at my grandmother's house. My great-grandmother lived with my grandmother and her husband. From the time I was a little girl to the time I was an adult, my great-grandmother prayed every single day at noon. Every day. So, when I would be there for the summer, I knew when twelve o'clock hit she would be like 'It's time to pray, come on,' so we would either pray together at twelve or she would pray by herself. She didn't care what was going on."

In her article "Black Family: Let's Pray Together," Kacie Starr Triplett writes about the importance of prayer in Black families and her own experience growing up: "I remember dating a young man in college whose family gathered in prayer as he and his siblings prepared to leave for college out of state. His parents demonstrated the leadership necessary to bring the family together for prayer; they had the wisdom and foresight to seek out God's protection and favor over their family. I grew up seeing my mother pray, and I knew she was praying on behalf of our family; however, prayer in our family was an individual act and not a collective one."[8]

Black girls today have had their own experiences with their families and prayer.

When I was younger, my grandma taught me this prayer that I have to say every night before I go to bed, and it's kind of engraved in my brain. And I feel guilty when I don't say it. "Now I go to bed at night, God keep me safe until morning light."—Paris, 18

I learned from my parents that prayer should be a conversation with God.—Erika, 13

My mom would always make us say, "Now I lay me down to sleep, I pray the Lord my soul to keep." We were like three years old. The end of it was terrifying now that I think of it. "If I shall die before I wake."—Jasmine, 15

While modern-day religious Black families don't necessarily pray three times per day as previous generations did, they find ways to practice prayer within everyday life.

My family, we pray at the end of the night to close the night. —Ashe, 13

In my family, when we have Sunday dinners, we pray before we eat. We also pray before we drive off for a road trip. —Cici, 15

Researchers Natalie Humphrey, Honore Hughes, and Deserie Holmes examined the concept of prayer from the perspective of Black children age eight to thirteen.[9] They argue that spirituality and religion have been socializing agents for many Black children. They found that "younger children were predicted to understand prayer as a ritual, while the older children were predicted to understand prayer to be more of a conversation."[10] This is very similar to my own experience growing up. I learned the practice of prayer at a young age, but as I grew older, I was taught that prayer was an important aspect of maintaining my relationship with God. Humphrey, Hughes, and Holmes's study also found that Black children conceptualize prayer as a personal ritual, a way to make requests on behalf of others, a way to give thanks, and a means to cope with difficult situations.

As a young Black girl, I was first taught that prayer is important. I may not have known why or how to pray, but I understood prayer to be both sacred and personal. The theology of prayer that I learned as a child focused on God. God was always at the center. In our God-centered prayers, we hoped to be transformed, to deepen our relationship with God, and to align ourselves with God's purpose. This is consistent with the theologies of prayer among the Black girls and women I spoke with.

You shouldn't rush to fit prayer into your schedule. You should have everything about God first and then your stuff.—Mae, 15

I used to think of prayer as this complicated essay. What do you say to God? Is he hearing you? What is happening? But now that I'm a teenager, it's like more of a conversation with God. So now I can speak my mind, and I know God hears me.—Tanya, 15

Similar to my own findings, 40 percent of participants in Humphrey, Hughes, and Holmes's study described prayer as a conversation. They interviewed a nine-year-old girl who explained her conversational approach to prayer, saying, "You could pray at night or anytime anywhere. . . . It's a conversation that I need to have with him at that moment."[11]

Some Black girls are confident that God hears their prayers, while others struggle with understanding the concept. They have questions about the nature of God, the role of divine intervention, and the general efficacy of prayer.

> *It's not that I don't understand prayer. It's more so I didn't feel much of a connection. My family always says, "Pray over it" or "Keep so-and-so in your prayers." I do think about it. I wonder if that makes me agnostic.—Lena, 17*

Some Black girls wonder how prayer is supposed to work, especially when it seems that some prayers are answered and others aren't. Seventeen-year-old Imani shared with me that she was in the car with her mother one day when her mother received a call from a friend who was sick. Imani's mother immediately started praying. Imani remembers sitting in the car watching her mother cry and pray on the phone with her friend. Imani sat in silence, not knowing how to react or what to say. For the next few months, Imani observed her mother praying constantly for her friend, but after six months her friend passed away. "I was like, I don't think all that praying worked. She's gone." Imani wondered, "Was the purpose to heal the woman? Is prayer about us getting our wish like magic?"

Seventeen-year-old Sarah grew up as an only child of a single mother. Though her mother had a job, she struggled to pay the bills, which continued to accumulate as time went on. "She tried to do what she could. She didn't have much money," Sarah shared. "It makes me emotional to talk about because she really did try her best." When she was twelve years old, Sarah and her mother were homeless for a year as their financial situation became dire. "During that phase of being homeless, my faith took a hit because I would pray that God would give us a home. We would go to the next home and the next hotel and the next place, and I doubted God." Sarah wishes she had documented that part of her life because she knows that her twelve-year-old self navigated real emotions that would be important to look back on now that she's older. "By the grace of God we got a new home when I was fourteen. But those few years were rough. I watched my mom crying, and I would scream at God, 'Where are you?'"

Sarah grew up believing in God, and that faith was passed on to her from her mother. "My mom kept praying. Despite it all, my mom believed Jesus would see us through." Sarah remembers that time as a test of her faith. "I think sometimes the way that God answers our prayers is not always the way we want. Sometimes it's in a way that I least expect. It may seem like he didn't answer them, but I think he just answered in a way I didn't think of. I realized that some things happen that we can't really explain even though I knew that God was near. Now we're in a home, and I realize that he was there the whole time."

The older I got, the more complicated prayer became. I was confused about how to pray in the aftermath of Norelle's murder or when my godbrother, Tye, was in the hospital for sickle cell anemia and the prognosis did not look good. I didn't always grasp the effectiveness of prayer. We were all concerned for Tye. I was just thirteen, and I specifically remember us fasting and praying. I did not know much about fasting, but I'd heard that when you wanted to reach God for a matter of urgency, you fasted. That was a scary time for me because someone I knew and was close to could possibly die, and I felt powerless. The only power that I felt I could lean on was the power of prayer. Tye eventually got better and was released from the hospital. At the time, I remember feeling this overwhelming sense of relief that our prayers worked, but I also realized that there would be many times when we would pray and there would be a different outcome.

Some Black girls believe in the efficacy of prayer. Humphrey, Hughes, and Holmes interviewed a ten-year-old girl who stated, "If somebody in her family is very sick, God can help her. To get rid of their problems and just think of something else and put their problems aside you do, and I think you should take everything to the Lord and he will do it."[12] However, other Black girls are more skeptical. Seventeen-year-old Saniyah simply said to me, "I just don't see the point if the Lord's will is going to happen anyway." Overall, Black girls seem to draw their own conclusions regarding answered and unanswered prayers. For the most part, they bring their own personal beliefs, experiences, and interpretations to prayer. For some, prayer is a means of coping with stress or finding comfort. Some pray for meaning or for guidance.

When I have a test, I'm calling on Jesus!—Chelsea, 14

I'll just be in my room and say, "Hey, God, what's up? I need a little bit of help right now. Thanks for whatever you send down. Amen."—Sienna, 13

Black girls who pray don't necessarily believe in formality when praying. They understand that prayer should be deeply personal and relational. This is similar to what former generations believed. They taught that God-centered prayer is a way to deepen our relationship with God. Spiritual Black girls have their own unique relationship with God.

I try to make a habit of praying in the morning and last thing at night. I've gotten in the habit of writing my prayers in my journal, kinda saying thank you for the day and for all God's done and the world. Gratitude prayers.—Lamaya, 16

When I was younger, I wasn't talking to God to get to know him; I was getting God to help me. But now it's not just what can I get. Now I'm just chatting about my day.—Jienna, 18

You can't physically see him. You can talk to him, but he's not gonna talk back. I mean, if he does talk back, then I'm outta here.—Lea, 16

Not all Black girls have the same confidence in prayer. Some feel disconnected from the spiritual practice for a variety of reasons, including doubt and skepticism, lack of meaning, or a general lack of belief.

To be 100 percent honest and transparent, my initial reaction to prayer is hesitancy.—Azaria, 14

When my family prays, I feel like they're more connected to God than me.—Dorcas, 16

I've prayed before, but it feels like talking to a wall sometimes. I've never had the real talking-to-God praying experience that other people have.—Clarise, 18

I felt like I was in the church because I was told. I feel like I was told that I should pray even though I didn't care to. —Salem, 18

Black girls' prayer lives do not all take the same form. While they have adopted some of the practices that were taught to them, Black girls find their own unique paths to connection with God and seeking meaning and spirituality. The girls I spoke with write in prayer journals and listen to prayer apps on their phones. Other girls don't pray often but make sure to say a prayer "from time to time" when they remember. Most of the Black girls mentioned gratitude as a prayer practice that they engage in often. "There is so much to be grateful for," Anisha said.

The Foundation of Prayer

When my aunt Heather was in hospice care, we gathered as a family around her bed as she awoke one morning. She spoke to us about how she'd slept and that she wasn't afraid because she knew she was going to be with the Lord. Then Aunt Heather said, "I would like Khristi to pray." It was a moment that still moves me to this day. I felt unprepared, humbled, and nervous. I was just in my twenties, and compared to other family members in the room, I was young and inexperienced. But for some reason Aunt Heather asked me to pray, and I did not take that request lightly. There would be many other moments when my family would look to me for prayer.

Another time when my family gathered at my parents' home for Thanksgiving, we stood in a circle around the table and one by one said what we were grateful for. When the last person was finished, it was time to pray. "Reverend," my dad said as he glanced at me. Everyone in the room looked over as though to concur that I should pray. It's funny how life has come full circle. As a little girl, I watched my grandmother on her knees praying to God, never quite sure what those moments meant but being engrossed by the devotion she had to God. I grew up watching my dad and uncle leading the family in prayer, usually as more of a spectator than a participant. And in church it was always the pastor, church mothers, or deacons who led the prayers.

To this day, it feels like a tremendous responsibility to lead my family in prayer. My personal prayer life fluctuates in the same complicated ways that it did when I was just a girl. I experience periods of inconsistency and changes in the depth of my prayer practices. There are times when I'm dedicated to a regular prayer routine and other times when life's demands or personal circumstances disrupt that routine. There are times when I'm more introspective and I seek spiritual connection or meaning. There are times when I pray for something and the opposite happens, and I find myself frustrated with God, and my prayer life is affected by that. Life is dynamic, and a fluctuating prayer life is a normal part of the spiritual journey. Regardless of where I am on that journey, I know that it is because of the foundation of prayer that I was given, that even though I might be distant at times, God is always near.

Woman*ish* Theology of Hospitality

How Black Girls Share Their Space

One summer day when I was five, my dad took me to lunch at the McDonald's on Flatbush Avenue in Brooklyn. It was one of the busiest parts of the borough, with lots of people shopping at the stores that lined the long street. As I left the restaurant, with my Happy Meal in one hand and my dad's hand in the other, I noticed a stuffed teddy bear on the ground. I paused and pulled my dad toward the bear. The bear was mangy, and its stuffing was not fluffy like that of store-bought bears. One of its eyes looked as though it had been scraped on cement. The left arm of the bear was torn open, and the cotton inside was coming out. Five-year-old me was devastated for the bear, all alone and abandoned in front of this busy McDonald's. My preschool mind did not understand how so many people could walk past this bear lying in the middle of the sidewalk. I feared that if we walked away no one would save the bear. I went to grab the bear, and my dad stopped me because it was dirty and of unknown origins. I begged my dad to let me take the bear home, which he agreed to, but he picked it up and told me we needed to wash it before I could have it.

As soon as we got home, I pestered my dad to wash the bear. I waited patiently while the bear was in the washing machine, and then we put the bear into the dryer, and I waited some more. When the dryer stopped, I took out the hot bear and sat with it in my room. *What should I name the bear?* I thought. I am not sure how long I sat there mulling over possible names, but I came up with the name Jason. "Your name will be Jason the Bear."

Our family was preparing to take our annual summer trip to Rocky Mount, North Carolina. I decided that I would take Jason with me, along with my pillow, which I named Coco. When the time came for us to pack the car, I sat in the back seat with Jason and Coco, ready for the long trip ahead. When we arrived at Rocky Mount, I showed Jason to Mama Hattie and told her about him. She sewed up his arm, and we searched in the attic among a bunch of old yard sale items for something for him to wear. We found a baby's T-shirt and put it on Jason. The shirt was a little big for Jason's frail frame, but we made it work. After we put the T-shirt on Jason, I felt that his rehabilitation was complete. Jason was my responsibility now, and I was relieved that I saved him and gave him a home.

I still have Jason to this day, sitting in my home with his sewed-up arm and that baby T-shirt on. My parents still marvel at how I had the mind to "save" the bear at that young age and have him even as an adult. I was a five-year-old embodying Jesus's directive, "For I was hungry and you gave me food, I was thirsty and you gave me something to drink, I was a stranger and you welcomed me, I was naked and you gave me clothing" (Matt. 25:35–36). I have no other way to describe it except that empathy was just within me somehow. Yet this was also a part of our family's philosophy and practice of loving our neighbor. My home was considered a home with a "revolving door," which meant that we always had a family member or visitor staying with us for an indefinite period of time.

My earliest memory of a family member staying with us is of Mama Hattie. When we first moved to New Jersey, she stayed with us for a few months to help with the transition. On one distinct occasion, I was playing with my Barbies a little too rough. Mama Hattie said, "You have to play nice with your dolls" and played with me to show me how even in imaginary play kindness was important.

Aunt Cynthia also stayed with us for a time. Aunt Cynthia was my father's sister. She was not much older than me and was just a teenager when she came. She was so young that my brother and I called her by her first name. At the time, I did not know why she came, but I later heard that she was having issues with my other grandmother. The reason why someone stayed with us was never a part of the conversation. My parents never sat us down to explain the presence of any guest. People simply came, and we made room for them. This taught me that the reason was neither here nor there. If someone needed a place to stay, and we had the space and the resources to provide them with a home, that was our responsibility.

To me, Cynthia was very cool. I considered her '90s cool, which meant that she had the admirable style of a '90s R&B artist. She owned so many pairs of colored Nike's and wore a different pair with each outfit. Her hair was always braided or pinned up in the latest styles. My mom was very happy when Cynthia came to stay with us because Mom didn't like doing my hair, and Cynthia was one of the best natural hair stylists. As much as I loved the outcome of my hair when she braided it, I did not love the process because I was "tender headed," meaning I had a sensitive scalp. I would cry my way through getting my hair braided, and Cynthia would be patient with me each time. While Cynthia stayed with us, she worked at TJ Maxx and got her GED. After a few years, she moved out on her own. She didn't move far away, but I was sad to see her go.

My cousin Tara came to stay with us shortly after. She was my uncle Greg's first daughter on my mom's side of the family. Tara was a student at Rutgers University, which was just a few miles from our house, so she would often stay with us on the weekends, and she lived with us in the summers while she worked a summer job. To me, Tara was brilliant. She went to Douglass College, an empowering, close-knit community within Rutgers that enhances the college experience for all majors by adding a feminist lens. Tara was an empowered young Black woman and my first real exposure to feminist ideals because she would often share what she was learning at school. She also came with us to church and considered herself a believer, so she had the mix of Christian and feminist thought that I would eventually adopt myself.

My cousin Ryan lived with my family twice. The first time he lived with us because he did not like his school in Washington, DC. He came when he was in the seventh grade but stayed only for that year. Ryan was the same age as my brother, Shaun, but they were opposites. At the time, Shaun was nerdish. Ryan, on the contrary, was a bit of a rebel. Shaun hung out with all the popular and studious kids. Ryan gravitated toward the troublemakers. Ryan and I had a lukewarm relationship. Sometimes we got along, and sometimes we did not. He often made fun of me, calling me "Oreo," accusing me of being dark on the outside but white on the inside. He made fun of the way I spoke, "like a White girl." He could be mean at times, and then I did not want to be around him. Other times we joked around and had fun. We treated him like any other member of our immediate family.

Ryan's time with us was short. He didn't connect well at the school he attended and spent time with the wrong crowds, so it was decided that it would be better if he went back to DC with my aunt Toxi. Later Ryan came back to live with us after getting into an altercation with some guys who were looking to kill him. He came to New Jersey and did a year of community college and eventually went back. It seemed like wherever Ryan went, he found trouble; he battled those same demons well into adulthood.

My aunt Veda also lived with us for many years. Aunt Veda had attended Howard University on a full scholarship and had graduated from Howard University Law School at the top of her class. She went on to practice law for many years and had a thriving life until the stress of her cases and the unaddressed trauma of her past caused her mental health to decline. Though I cannot recall her exact diagnosis, I always thought she had dissociative identity disorder. I remember one time I came home from basketball practice, went into the kitchen, and said, "Hey, Aunt Veda!" In an Italian accent, she responded, "My name is not Veda. It is Vitali." I simply shrugged my shoulders and said, "Okay. Hey, Vitali." I went to the refrigerator, grabbed a snack, and went to my room without thinking anything was odd about the exchange. To my teenaged self, this was normal. Sometimes Aunt Veda would sit in the living room and chuckle and speak to herself as though she were having a conversation with someone. Aunt Veda's mental state was not discussed in depth with us. My mother and her siblings communicated often and took care of Aunt Veda, but I don't remember being included in family meetings or being told what was happening. At times it felt like the adults wanted us children to think that she was just fine, but I knew that was not the case.

I did appreciate the way my family was patient and grace-giving with Aunt Veda. There were times of normalcy when she was on her meds, went to therapy, and had a daily routine. During one of those times, Aunt Veda got a job working for a local newspaper as a delivery person. One day she asked me to spend time with her on a route, and I agreed, not knowing it meant waking up at four o'clock in the morning. Still, driving around East Brunswick watching the sun rise as we threw newspapers out the car window is one of my fondest memories. Aunt Veda saved money, got a car, and helped out our family by getting groceries or driving me to basketball practices when my parents were working. She even taught me to drive after I got my permit; the time she spent showing me how to parallel park helped me pass my driver's test. My senior year in high school, Aunt Veda's mental health took a decline, and she eventually went back to Rocky Mount to stay with Aunt Mary.

My mom and dad believed that we always take care of family, no matter the circumstance. Bad or good. Deserving or not. As a young Black girl, I was taught that our lives, our homes, and our churches should be places where everyone feels welcome. My upbringing in my family and my church formed my theology of hospitality. It helped me develop a way of thinking about the world and the nature of God. In hospitality, we extend invitations to strangers, friends, and family. In service, we build a more humane and just society.

Black Girls Gathering

On a cool September day, thirteen teenaged Black girls come pouring through my door out of the rain. "Shoes off please!" I say. "Chick-fil-A's in the dining room." "Thank you!" they exclaim one after another as they take off their shoes and head straight for the food. It has been a few weeks since we started back at the boarding school where I work. And this is our first "Black Girls Gathering" of the school year: a name a few girls who'd graduated six years prior came up with. The boarding school's students not only receive academic instruction but also live on the school's campus for extended periods of time, typically weeks or months at a stretch. Like other predominantly White institutions, our school has historically had a predominantly White student body, faculty, and administration, though in recent years efforts to increase diversity and to create an inclusive environment have been ongoing. As one of only a small number of Black faculty, I serve as a mentor and adviser to many of the school's Black students, and in particular the Black girls.

I always have my eye on how the Black girls are doing, emotionally, socially, and academically. Because they spend so much time here, this campus and school are home away from home for them, which can be hard when they have little adult representation and are small in number. Like me, the older Black girls pay attention to who arrives. They introduce themselves to the new Black girls whenever they get the opportunity. They exchange numbers and social media information to stay in touch. They let the new girls know that they are there for them whenever they need, and they give them advice on how to exist in a space where they are so few. There is no official practice or ordinance for their graciousness; this is merely something that is innate within the girls. "Looking out for other people is like you're looking out for yourself," Jasmine, who is a junior this school year, told me. This is the essence of hospitality: providing warmth, kindness, and genuine concern for the well-being of those around us. The older girls want the younger girls to feel "at home," even though they are away from the homes they know.

When I first arrived at the school, as the only Black woman faculty member, I felt obligated to spend time with the Black girls. It was their idea to have gatherings at my home. It was their idea to officially name our time together "Black Girls Gathering." This gave them a chance to spend intentional time with one another and to get to know some of the younger girls who were new to the school. I had no idea that this would become a treasured tradition that we would experience several times a year. Black Girls Gathering has never felt like a part of my job on campus. Instead, I feel it is my responsibility to these girls. I am intentional about them meeting in my home and not just any other space on campus because the act of opening my home demonstrates the spiritual practice of hospitality that I was taught as a young girl. In this space, a teaching and learning component takes place as I practice hospitality with the girls and the girls practice hospitality with one another.

My heart is so full whenever the girls come over. We have no agenda. I usually have a meal or dessert waiting for them, and they sit together and eat. They play with one another's hair and make TikTok videos and post selfies. They are a loud, rambunctious group and love to laugh and joke with one another. This makes me particularly happy because in my mind their joy means they are comfortable in my space. Whenever a person feels "at home," it usually means they feel at ease simply being their natural selves.

"I really like your home. The artwork is really nice," Shari says. She's a new student, and this is her very first Black Girls Gathering.

"Thank you," I respond. "When I was growing up, my parents always had African artwork around our house, so I try to keep that same feel in my own home."

"Cool," Shari says.

Alumni Black girls paved the way for these younger girls, and the thought crosses my mind that this has become somewhat of a ministry for me and for them. I ask Shari how she has felt welcomed by the older Black girls here.

> If the older girls weren't here, my experience here would be awkward. I still remember convocation, when I first saw Dami, Nicole, and Lola. I immediately thought, *I'm gonna go talk to them.* I'm the only Black girl in my dorm. Meeting them helped me get acclimated faster. Older girls who have been in the space for a while have experiences. They can answer questions that you don't want to ask others who can't relate. I remember early in the year we went to the Grille and we talked for almost two hours just about the Black community and Black space here. That was something that was so important to me.

Keila, an older student, beams with pride while Shari responds to my question. I ask Keila why she is smiling, and she tells me about the time she saw Shari in the background of a picture. "One of my friends sent me a snap, and I was like 'Oh, who's that?' She told me who it was, and I said, 'I'm going to need to meet her because she's another one of us.' Then I met her, and she was really nice. We're friends now."

"Do you see it as your responsibility to be hospitable to the younger Black girls coming in?" I ask Keila.

"It's my responsibility to try to get to know everyone in our community and make them feel welcome like I was when I was new. There are not a lot of us. The first people I met on campus weren't Black, and that was fine. But it was hard not seeing anyone who looked like me. But I remember coming to my first Black Girls Gathering, and that helped me to know there are more of us."

At each gathering, I spend the first few moments with the girls after they arrive, but then I retreat upstairs while they hang out with one another in the living room. I want them to know that I trust them in my home and that my home is literally their home as well, which means that I behave the way I would if they lived in the space. They can grab something to drink from the refrigerator or watch TV or gossip. On this particular night, they decide to spend time in my third-floor loft area. After being upstairs for just a few minutes, I hear a series of loud thumps.

"What are you ladies doing up there?" I yell.

"We're just practicing our cartwheels!"

I have always just wanted them to feel relaxed and at home. Mission accomplished.

In her book *Dear Sisters: A Womanist Practice of Hospitality*, N. Lynne Westfield argues that religious education "would benefit greatly from a refocus, based on a sacramental understanding of hospitality, as modeled by concealed gatherings of Christian African-American women."[1] She believes that Black women's practice of gathering provides a theological model of hospitality. This model provides a framework for understanding and practicing hospitality as a spiritual discipline deeply connected to one's faith. Pastor Mary Anderson writes, "If the theology of hospitality is to create a welcome environment where the word of God is more easily heard and understood, then we must always be attentive to what people need so that their eyes, ears, hearts and minds are open to the Spirit of God."[2]

When Black women gather and practice hospitality, it is a source of healing, renewal, and resilience. Westfield's writing, along with the Black Girls Gatherings, has provided me with a framework to understand the practices of hospitality embraced by Black girls as their own form of resistance. Westfield asserts that Black women gather as a ritual of resilience in the face of dehumanization, and in my experience, Black girls do the same. For *Dear Sisters*, Westfield interviewed Black women who shared their perspectives on the joys and nuances of their gathering practice. One interviewee, Delores Marshall, said, "It's just a sisterhood there and it's a warm feeling. We know that we can talk about anything. We can say anything. We can talk about our husbands. We're joking about them. But it's a love there that we are talking about. . . . It's an understanding that we have our own kind of vocabulary. And we have our own kind of understanding. Whereas if there were someone else in there, it would be cold. We wouldn't talk openly or freely. We have a good time at our meetings."[3]

I ask sixteen-year-old Aarika how she feels about our Black Girls Gathering. "There's not many of us. And I think like Tosh is even the only Black girl in her grade. So, we have to stick together. There's no room for competition because we're all we've got. When I'm here, I don't have to explain myself. We get each other. I always have to be so careful with what I say when I'm around White people—students or teachers. It's exhausting."

Westfield describes her Dear Sisters Literary Group that formed in 1995. Women from their late twenties to their seventies meet monthly in one another's homes for conversation and book discussion. They share a meal and one another's joyous company. "The women of the group engage in banterous conversation throughout the evening gatherings," she writes.[4] Westfield says that their time together offers them intentional hospitality in the form of concealed gatherings. "Concealed gatherings," she writes, "away from Whites and African-American men, are powerful events for African-American women filled with food, laughter, and deadly serious moments of healing, release, and relaxation."[5]

Hospitality is about making people feel welcome, comfortable, and valued. Hospitality is the work of God. The Greek term for hospitality can be translated as "guest-friendship" or "love of strangers." There are examples of men and women being hospitable throughout the Old and New Testaments, and Scripture encourages us to be hospitable toward one another. Hospitality is a fundamental vocation of humanness. We tend to God by tending to one another.

Westfield references Henri Nouwen's definition of hospitality, which is evocative of the hospitality practices of Black women and girls. In his book *Reaching Out*, Nouwen writes, "In our world, full of strangers, estranged from their own past, culture and country, from their neighbors, friends and family, from their deepest self, and their God, we witness a painful search for a hospitable place, where life can be lived without fear, and where community can be found."[6] He says that Old and New Testament stories "show how serious our obligation is to welcome the stranger in our home."[7]

The Old Testament contains several instances in which hospitality is encouraged and instances in which people are instructed on how they are to treat strangers in their land. In the New Testament, Jesus and his disciples often rely on the hospitality of others during their ministry. The apostle Paul also writes about hospitality in his letters. Hospitality is valued as a virtuous practice in the Bible, and it reflects the principles of love, compassion, and caring for others that are central to Jesus's teachings. Westfield writes, "Hospitality is a host's friendly sharing of resources for the comfort of a guest. Of equal or greater importance, hospitality is the genuine, uninhibited sharing of self: spontaneous laughter, rest, reassurance, comfort, and familiarity. Hospitality is an attitude."[8] Hospitality is a spiritual practice when it is approached with a deep sense of mindfulness, compassion, and a desire to connect with others on a profound level. Black women and girls may not intentionally approach hospitality with a spiritual mindset, but their hospitality is grounded in selflessness, compassion, and interconnectedness, which are spiritual principles. "As a strategy for resilience, African American women carve out a niche of intimacy through such gatherings where they have neither to defend nor to deny their place or their humanness."[9]

In *Parable of the Brown Girl*, I write about the Becoming Conference. During the day, I would set aside space in the schedule for the girls to spend time together apart from the regular programming. "Every year during these times, the girls choose to listen to music, dance, take selfies and photos of one another, and just spend time together in general. The room is typically very loud with girls conversing and laughing. Their loudness is *how* they have a good time together and how they express their love for one another. In these moments, their loudness is not a defense mechanism or a plea to be heard, but rather a shared love language."[10] When Black girls gather, the sacred space of hospitality toward one another has an atmosphere of healing.

Black girls are hospitable in ways that extend beyond their social circles. When Blair was in the sixth grade, her teacher moved her assigned seat to another area of class. She didn't know why and wasn't concerned about it but told her mother. Her mother emailed the teacher to ask why Blair had been moved. Blair's teacher explained that she had noticed how kind and courteous Blair had been to two other students in class: one was disabled and in a wheelchair, and the other was a boy with Tourette syndrome. Out of twenty-five students, Blair was the only student who had made friends with both students, and she had taken it upon herself to help them when they needed it. Other students in the class overlooked the two boys, and at times they felt ostracized, but Blair treated them as friends. She moved Blair to where she could be close to both boys. The teacher noted what she called Blair's "hospitable leadership."

Fourteen-year-old Talia shared a story about a classmate she'd gotten a gift for one day. "One of my classmates, I wasn't really close to her at all, but she was very nice. We happened to be talking after class and she was telling me how her birthday was coming up and she was saying that her family was having money problems so she wouldn't be getting anything for her birthday. I thought about that. So, I told my parents that I was going to get something for her. It was small, but she was so happy when I gave it to her. I just wanted her to feel good about herself."

Hospitality invites everyone to the table. Hospitality extends community to all, regardless of privilege. Hospitality is treating everyone how God treats us: with an open invitation to kindness.

Blessed Hospitality

Without knowing it, many modern-day Black girls express a theology of hospitality in their everyday practices as individuals and as a community. I am grateful to have been exposed to a culture of radical hospitality in my girlhood. My family and my church refused to turn away those in need. Everyone was welcome: friend, family, or stranger. Hospitality can take many forms, from invitations to homes to caring for people of any community. Hospitality is about recognition and acceptance.

I remember as a teenager witnessing a radical act of hospitality one day at church. There had been a robbery at a gas station that had resulted in the shooting of its owner, a Hindu man. The gas station was located just a few blocks from the church. That Sunday Pastor Buster Soaries shared what happened and said that we focus so much attention on violence done to our own cultural community that we fail to notice when those of other ethnicities and religions are affected by crime. Our church took up an offering for the medical bills and any other financial needs that the victim and his family may have had. After taking up the collection, we proceeded with the rest of the service.

After the benediction, Rev. Soaries said that we were going to march as a congregation from the church to the gas station. We gathered outside the church and then sang hymns on the way there. The man who owned the station was still in the hospital, but his family was there managing things. I remember that when they came outside their faces were full of pleasant surprise. Rev. Soaries gave them the money we had collected, and we prayed with them. He told them that even though we weren't the same religion we were still family, and we were part of the same community.

This was a significant teaching moment for me as a teenager. This was an instance in which we didn't invite people to our church or our house. We extended ourselves to them in their space. I learned that hospitality should extend beyond people in our circle. I learned that hospitality should extend to those God puts before us. I was just a young Black girl observing this example of hospitality, but it spoke an essential message to me. The practice of hospitality is rooted in Scripture and should be manifested in us. The purpose of our blessedness is to bless others. This was one of many moments when I saw the gospel and Scripture exemplified.

Woman*ish* Theology of Service

How Black Girls Love Their Neighbors

Nothing gives my dad more joy than serving. This is his ministry to God. He is the personification of Matthew 6:3–4, where Jesus instructs his disciples, "When you give alms, do not let your left hand know what your right hand is doing, so that your alms may be done in secret, and your Father who sees in secret will reward you." He serves not for the reward but for the pleasure of service and service alone. I grew up watching both my parents exemplify a theology of service daily.

At First Baptist, my dad was a deacon and my mom was a deaconess, and they were a part of what we called the diaconate ministry. I was a proud deacon's kid (DK) and made friends with other DKs. Next to the senior pastor, the diaconate held a great deal of power in the church. As volunteers, they were responsible for serving and meeting the practical needs of the church and community. They served as the main support and chief advisers for the pastor. They led worship, conducted baptisms, took in prospective members, taught Sunday school, assisted with pastoral care, and helped people in the community with financial needs. My parents would sometimes drop my siblings and me off at home after church, and then they would go out together to serve Communion to and visit some of the sick and shut-in members, or those people in nursing homes, in the hospital, or physically unable to attend services. My parents would pray with them, encourage them, and bring them whatever they needed.

My dad was also one of the deacons in charge of our benevolence ministry. The benevolence ministry offered financial assistance and other practical help to individuals and families in need within the church and the broader community. Our church would have a special benevolence offering on Sundays that people would donate to, and my dad would manage how those funds were used. Oftentimes, my dad would meet with people who didn't have money to pay rent or other utilities. Some people were in medical debt or were close to foreclosure. My dad wouldn't just give them money but would offer counseling and personal support as well. He took pride in being responsible for the benevolence ministry. He loved helping people. "Somebody needed to pay their rent or their electric bill," he said to me as he reflected on his years in ministry. "A lot of lights were off. Folks needed money. In New Jersey, when school was out for the summer, teachers and other school personnel—people who worked in the cafeteria—didn't get paid. So a lot of those folks came to the church for help. We gave about $125,000 a year in help. Even churches who were in trouble would come to us for help."

On one occasion, a family from a town a distance from the church needed money for a funeral because they did not have insurance. They needed $3,000 to bury their son. My dad took the money to the funeral home to hand-deliver it.

On another occasion, in March 1994, a natural gas pipeline exploded in Edison, New Jersey, and destroyed 128 apartments. It was the largest pipeline explosion of its kind in a highly populated area. In addition to local authorities and the pipeline company, our church came together to help those displaced. "It uprooted a lot of families, and we just had to help," my dad told me. Another time there was a fire on Christmas Day at an apartment complex across the street from the church, and I recall my dad helping mobilize church members to come up with a plan to help.

Our church's motto was "Faith in Action," based on James 2:14–17, which says, "What good is it, my brothers and sisters, if someone claims to have faith but does not have works? Surely that faith cannot save, can it? If a brother or sister is naked and lacks daily food and one of you says to them, 'Go in peace; keep warm and eat your fill,' and yet you do not supply their bodily needs, what is the good of that? So faith by itself, if it has no works, is dead." "Faith in Action" was in our logo, on the church walls, and on church T-shirts to remind our church community of our mission. I witnessed our congregation and leadership serving at every level, from providing financial literacy and job training to people in the community to partnering with the Department of Children and Families in placing children in the foster-care system into homes. First Baptist Church was also responsible for purchasing housing developments for low-income people, creating violence prevention programs, and creating educational initiatives for underrepresented children. We would help with food drives and give away food. We had a Thanksgiving turkey drive and gave away hundreds of turkeys for years. Pastor Buster Soaries also bought a local building and created the First Baptist Community Development Corporation (FBCDC) in the mid-1990s. FBCDC eventually became the home of our foster-care agency called Harvest of Hope, employment readiness programs, and a youth development center. These were all services that First Baptist provided not just to our church members but to the entire community. Our church was constantly in service to others.

My dad was known as the deacon to go to when people needed help. His penchant for service was an extension of my grandfather's influence. We called my grandfather "Dede," and Dede, like my dad, was a deacon. Dede was an electrician by trade, and he did a lot of physical work in the church. My dad remembers that clearly. "In those days, the church couldn't afford to hire anyone to help with the building. The officers in the church did the work. Black folks couldn't even hire snow removal companies back in those days. The deacons did that work." Dede would have my dad help with some of the work in the church when he was a boy.

Mom and Dad served in those positions for over thirty years, beginning at Bethany Baptist Church in Brooklyn and continuing when we moved to New Jersey. Their service and hospitality were not limited to the church or our home; they extended into every area of their lives. When I think on their service, I am also reminded of the passage in Matthew 25 where the king says, "Come, you who are blessed by my Father, inherit the kingdom prepared for you from the foundation of the world, for I was hungry and you gave me food, I was thirsty and you gave me something to drink, I was a stranger and you welcomed me, I was naked and you gave me clothing, I was sick and you took care of me, I was in prison and you visited me" (vv. 34–37). When the righteous people wonder when they did this to the king, he responds, "Truly I tell you, just as you did it to one of the least of these brothers and sisters of mine, you did it to me" (v. 40).

My mom's passion for service was also shown in her work as a teacher. She worked at New Brunswick High School as a special education administrator. I would often go to the school to visit my mom and her students. For some reason, I felt cool being around them and felt even cooler being the daughter of the teacher all the students gravitated to. "Mrs. Adams, this your daughter?" students would ask as I sat in my mom's classroom, where students would stop by all day to hang out or talk or eat their lunch. They were all so attached to her, and for good reason. Besides teaching, my mother was a class adviser.

She played a crucial role in supporting students' academic, personal, social, and emotional development.

However, my mother's service to her students went beyond her job description. She provided a supportive and empathetic presence throughout their educational journey. She served her students and was fully committed to their overall well-being and personal growth. "Students became my family," she told me. "It wasn't just about teaching them; it was about helping to provide for them socially and emotionally. A lot of them had emotional issues and financial circumstances that prevented them from having the things they needed. And you never knew what was going on in their homes."

When the father of one of her students passed away and the family did not have enough money to pay for the funeral, my mother raised money for the funeral. There were times when a family's electricity was turned off and my mother would help pay their bill. One student came from a financially poor family and was raised by her grandmother. This student had some personal hygiene issues, and my mother brought toiletries to her. My mother would take her clothes to the laundry in between classes and would have them back to her, cleaned, by the end of the day. My mother would help students get school supplies and would give them rides to and from school. I also recall when it came time for prom that my mother took some of the girls to Macy's to help them buy prom dresses.

These things were natural to me. I didn't see them as service. I just saw my mother helping students any way she could. It was just a part of what she did. A lot of that came from her mama and her upbringing.

Both my parents believed that it was our responsibility to look out for anyone in need. This was a theological belief that they carried out in their personal lives.

Never Disconnected from the Community

My friend Kim Copeland is an ordained minister and active in serving the community around her. Growing up as a Black girl with a father and mother whose servant leadership was based in the church and community, she had an experience similar to my own. "Their teaching was always 'We are a part of a community,'" she told me. That informed Kim's own theology of service as a Black girl. "As a kid, serving was never not a part of my life."

Kim's dad grew up in the inner city and was considered a prodigy. He went to Harvard and upon graduating went back to the Black community in Cleveland. Kim said, "The first thing he did was run for public office." Her father often helped people with legal matters and used his academic experience to help the community and the church. Eventually, he became a deacon in the church.

Her mother worked in the corporate field but also had a heart for youth and education. Kim said that her mom used her career to help open doors for young people in the community. "She was determined to make sure every Black and Brown child had access to education." Her mother was also active in the church, and Kim has vivid memories of her mom "jumping in when there was a challenge or a tragedy in the church and community." Service in both the church and the community was a natural part of who they were as a family. Kim said she believes that her family's theology of service goes back generations. "I would hear stories about my great-grandmother, who registered people to vote in the church. My grandmother was a teacher who was invested in making a difference in the lives of young people."

Kim's parents made sure she grew up with the teachings on service that had been passed down through their family over the years. Not only did they teach her about service, but they also made sure she was involved in clubs and organizations that were service oriented. In church, Kim participated in service projects and volunteered in food kitchens. "There were many opportunities for service growing up. My family made sure I was involved."

As a young Black girl, Kim witnessed her parents' service, which had a big influence on who she is today. Kim's career and ministry are built on that foundation. "I use all my gifts and access for the benefit of the community. There is never a sense of being disconnected from the community. It's just who I am, and I always have the mindset of being available for the next moment."

An Innate Theology of Service

Not all Black girls grow up with parents who are models of servant leadership. Yet service often comes naturally to many Black girls who approach situations with a focus on helping and providing value to others. Many Black girls are simply attentive to the needs and concerns of others. Within them is an innate theology of service that we can learn from.

A theology of service guides individuals and communities to engage in acts of service, compassion, and justice based on their religious or spiritual beliefs. Service means engaging in an activity that is aimed primarily at supporting others without an expectation of personal gain or recognition in return. It is very similar to hospitality, with its theme of being welcoming. Service is the action that typically follows or runs alongside hospitality. The underlying principle is the same for both: dedicating oneself to helping others as an expression of one's faith and commitment to the well-being of others. Service is a way for people to live out their faith in a practical and compassionate manner. Black girls are natural servant leaders. They are genuinely concerned about the welfare of others. They have a deep commitment to serve others. They have natural gifts for fostering community. They possess humility and self-awareness.

Giving and service are my biggest spiritual callings. It's nothing for me to serve. I enjoy it. I like helping other people because I've been so blessed, and giving a little part of me to somebody else isn't a hard thing for me.—Haleemah, 17

I grew up with the Christian message that your money isn't yours, and I took it wholeheartedly and I'm not even mad about that. If I have money, I will give it to the first cause of a person in need that I can. I have always been someone who loves to serve. I'm learning how to balance it.—Candice, 15

"My mom always told me, 'Have an eye for where there is a deficit,'" seventeen-year-old Allegra told me. Essentially, this means having a keen sense of observation and being attuned to the needs of others. Allegra has taken the message to heart. It inspires her to always pay attention to areas where she can be helpful. For example, she recently created a diversity club at school "because there are few BIPOC students" there, and she believes there is a need for community among the students of color at her school.

Black girls are always filling in the spaces where there are gaps. They see where there is a need, and they work to meet it. A fifth-grader named Chloe started a recycling club at her school simply because she felt there was too much wasted paper. "I needed to help the planet. I was very passionate about it," she said. Jaelyn is a senior at her high school, and when she was in the tenth grade, she started a girls' mentoring group that meets every Wednesday morning. "We talk about different things like body positivity and social issues," she said. "I give advice. I want to remind them that they're enough and important. Their voice matters. It's important to me because of how much I know I needed that as a young girl."

Another young activist with a larger platform is Mari Copeny, who became a vocal advocate for the people affected by the water crisis in Flint, Michigan. Her dedication to her community and her advocacy for clean water have made her a symbol of resilience and activism, especially among young people. In my book *Unbossed: How Black Girls Are Leading the Way*, I write about Ssanyu

Lukoma, who started a literacy organization at twelve years of age when she came to the realization that many kids in her age group did not have the opportunity to read diverse literature. "God gave me purpose. My purpose is to lead. My purpose is to inspire people," she said. I also tell about sixteen-year-old Grace Callwood, who was diagnosed with non-Hodgkin lymphoma as a child. Not long after receiving her diagnosis, a friend told her about a family with two young girls who had lost their home in a fire. "All I could think of was that I had just entered sickness and they had just entered homelessness," Grace remembers. While she was still receiving her own medical treatment, Grace decided to donate the clothes she could no longer wear to the two girls. When Grace heard about how happy the girls were to receive the clothes, she knew she wanted to do more. Grace is now the founder of the We Cancerve Foundation, whose mission is to bring happiness to children who are homeless, sick, or in foster care. She lives according to her own personal motto: "There is no age limit on service."[1]

Black girls are serving in public and private spaces. They seek to create positive environments where anyone they welcome into their lives feels comfortable and valued. They often serve in what they feel are small ways, but even these actions have lasting, positive effects. Black girls having a sense of responsibility and serving the community around them is nothing new. Historically, Black women have made significant contributions in service to society. Black women have been serving in the church and community for decades. "Through their churches,

African American women throughout the twentieth century founded clubs, national political organizations, and local charitable institutions. Their work provided scholarships for students, meals for the hungry, training for the unemployed, and advocacy for the community."[2] Black girls are continuing in the tradition of their foremothers by exhibiting a similar theology of service rooted in love and generosity.

> *It doesn't take a lot out of me to serve. I've worked ten-hour volunteer days, and my mom's like "Are you not tired?" and I'm like "I made somebody smile, so I'm okay."—Nikki, 16*

Fifteen-year-old Kendra volunteers at a community center that provides programming for youth, their families, and the community. After school she walks over to the community center and spends three hours with elementary- and middle-school students. "Most of the kids who go have parents who are working or who can't take care of them after school," she told me. Kendra usually stays until the very last kid has left the building, even though she's not required to stay that long. While there she helps the kids with homework, plays games with them, or makes TikTok videos with them on her phone. If any of them needs advice, Kendra is there to be a listening ear and to offer her wisdom. Kendra is still young herself, but with them she feels like an overprotective big sister. She loves what she calls "being a bridge for them." She wants to point them in the right direction in life and uses every opportunity to encourage them. She never hesitates to let them know that they're destined for greatness in life. This is her mission and calling, which she is just recently discovering. "My area of service is younger kids. I like for them to know what they're capable of. I just realized this about myself. I enjoy being a mentor and giving advice." Her mission and the bond she has built with the young students keep her coming back each day.

The program paused during the summer while school was out, and it had been a while since Kendra had been at the community center. One day she saw two of her students while shopping with her mom. "It was so sweet they remembered me. One of the kids is named Montana. He pretends to hate me, but he loves me. He said, 'I can still beat you in eight-ball.' That made me really happy. I couldn't believe they remembered. I can't wait to go back."

> *I have always been a giving person. Almost to the detriment of myself.—Alese, 16*

Black women and girls have a natural sense of obligation to their communities and families; however, this can come at a cost to their well-being. Like many Black women, Black girls can overcommit or take on more responsibilities or obligations than they can reasonably handle or manage effectively. They are sometimes stretched thin or overwhelmed in their giving.

While I learned a healthy theology of service from my parents, some Black girls aren't as fortunate. Seventeen-year-old Pia has mixed feelings about how Black women give of themselves based on what she saw her mother do.

> Service is an interesting thing because my mom—I've seen her give so much to our family. Most of the time I didn't look at it as something admirable because I saw how much it stressed her out. I've never seen her accept nice things for herself. She would always say, "Someone else could use this money." Seventy-five percent of her shopping is getting things for other people. She's paid for my cousins' schools. These are obviously nice things she's doing. But she's not appreciated. I'm not completely turned off to service, but this has taught me to be cautious.

Pia mentioned that her mother is a religious woman and sees her giving as part of her "service to God." Pia said her mother is like "Martha being too busy," referring to a passage in Luke 10. In the passage, a woman named Martha welcomes Jesus into her home and is busy with the cooking and serving. In contrast, her sister Mary sits at Jesus's feet listening to his teachings. Martha becomes frustrated and asks Jesus to tell Mary to help with the chores. However, Jesus gently rebukes Martha, saying that Mary has chosen the better path.

Many interpretations of this passage focus on prioritizing one's relationship with Jesus over worldly distractions. Martha was preoccupied with the practical tasks of serving and hospitality. However, it could have been that Martha's service to Jesus *was* her prioritizing her relationship with him. So many Black women and girls see service as their mission and calling. Pia's observation is that this type of thinking without the proper boundaries can be detrimental. Perhaps Pia realizes that Black women and girls who have a commitment to service need to be a bit more like Mary. She understands that the desire to serve others is a positive and valuable quality but that it is essential to strike a balance to prevent it from becoming detrimental to one's well-being. Still, Pia's mother taught her "to be a giver. When you've done well for yourself, then you go to help others, especially when it comes to family." Service involves personal sacrifice and humility. True service is selfless.

> *I've heard the language of service all my life from my mom, so what I do is sort of in a way reinforcing what I learned at home.—Jenee, 15*

Overall, Black girls understand the concept of service as being integral to their growth and development. They see service as helping them grow to become better human beings. Service can cultivate qualities within them such as empathy, resilience, and self-awareness while providing a sense of purpose and fulfillment. Ultimately, they realize that serving others leads to a more enriched and meaningful life.

> *I think I'm growing, and as I grow, I share what I've learned with other people.—Harper, 18*
>
> *I've seen the benefits that it's given me and others to fully engage in service when given the opportunities.—Gigi, 16*

Black girls are also self-aware. They approach their service with a spirit of humility. Many check their motives to make sure they are not serving with selfish intent. Sometimes service can lead people to have a savior complex, in which they believe they are the saviors or heroes who can single-handedly solve the problems of those they are trying to help. Black girls' service is often rooted in humility, and they are open to learning and growth at the same time.

You cannot let your own ambitions get in the way of being a selfless and kind person.—India, 16

I think of myself as a selfless person, but I also know I can be selfish with my own ambitions. So I'm trying to work on that.—Shamea, 17

God has given me the ability to do certain things, and I feel like it would be selfish if I didn't share that to help someone else. What I'm doing is for more than just me.—Lauren, 14

In *Unbossed*, I write about Marian Wright Edelman, the founder and president of the Children's Defense Fund, who once said, "Service is the rent we pay for being. It is the very purpose of life, and not something you do in your spare time."[3] Black girls come from generations of Black women who had natural gifts for service leadership. This service leadership has always been rooted in a desire to serve communities as opposed to gaining power.

Faith in Action

I visited a church one Sunday, and the pastor of the congregation preached a sermon on serving the Lord with gladness. With passion and fervent enthusiasm, he spoke to the congregation: "There ought to be some gladness that God would use somebody like us! I'm talking about serving the Lord with gladness because some of us used to serve the devil real good. But God saved our lives, cleaned us up, and we ought to be serving the Lord. This is how we give thanks! How do we give thanks? By serving!"

I made it a point to observe the Black girls sitting in the pew next to me. There were four of them wearing their Sunday dresses with their hair in sections and bows. They couldn't have been more than ten years old. They were paying attention and looking up at the adults near them, mimicking their clapping and shouting as the pastor preached. At the end of the sermon, the pastor spoke about an initiative the congregation could engage in to help the migrant crisis in New York and those who had been displaced. "You can have your opinion about policy, but as a church we have a responsibility." He told the congregation they must be loving toward "those who are seeking shelter in another area because that is the story of our Savior." He probably said the word *responsibility* almost a dozen times as he spoke.

I wondered how the girls in that congregation were processing what they were hearing. I supposed their womanish theology of service was being formed. As you listen to sermons emphasizing responsibility and witness your faith community engaging in acts of service, the significance of this concept is bound to resonate with you eventually. It certainly did with me. I thought back on the hundreds of sermons I'd heard in my own girlhood. Hearing that

"God loves a cheerful giver" and Scripture passages about serving the Lord with a joyful heart formed a theology of service in my young psyche even though I did not realize it.

During my senior year in high school, my English teacher told us to write an essay about our future careers. The assignment seemed to come easy to my classmates. I felt like everyone knew exactly what they wanted to do with their lives. My friend Andre wanted to go into hospitality management. Another friend wanted to be an engineer. I could not confidently identify what I wanted to do. I didn't want to be a doctor or lawyer. I knew I wanted to help people, so I researched helping professions. I looked into social work, psychology, even physical therapy. Still, I wasn't sure what form my helping would take. I was just certain that I wanted to have a positive impact on the world around me.

Perhaps this unction to help was formed in those early years when I observed my mom and dad consistently reflect kindness, compassion, and a willingness to contribute to the well-being and betterment of others. Perhaps it was formed as I saw my church play a significant role in serving and empowering the community. Perhaps it was formed as I was a part of a congregation that advocated for social justice and equity and provided youth and economic development programs, counseling, job placement services, and a plethora of other services for community members in need. Service was as ingrained in my theology and practice as it was in my psyche. For this I am grateful to have had both the example of Jesus in Scripture and the examples of my family and church around me.

My high school self could not articulate why my heart guided me to service. I did not realize that service was my vocation. I just wanted to dedicate my life to serving others and making a positive impact on the world. It's just who I was.

Conclusion

> Even if there is no single, universal, black female experience, there are enough shared identities, beliefs, and experiences to offer insight into African American women as a group.
>
> —Melissa Harris-Perry, *Sister Citizen: Shame, Stereotypes, and Black Women in America*

Can I share my own thoughts about God?" thirteen-year-old Saniyah asked me.

"Yes," I responded, "you absolutely can."

Listening to the theological perspectives of Black girls can point us straight to God. In *Parable of the Brown Girl*, I write, "In Matthew 18, Jesus calls a little child over to him and the disciples, saying, 'Truly I tell you, unless you change and become like little children, you will never enter the kingdom of heaven.' Perhaps this is what God is doing with black girls—placing them in our lives to remind us to be as vulnerable, unprejudiced, adaptable, and benevolent as they are. To get closer to God, we must become like them."[1]

I echo similar sentiments here. To get closer to God, we must listen to the unique experiences, perspectives, and cultural insights that Black girls bring to theological discussions. It's important to create spaces and opportunities for Black girls to engage in theology and contribute to the ongoing exploration of our own faith and spirituality. Black girls can offer fresh interpretations of religious texts, traditions, and doctrines. Aside from this, the thoughts, emotions, and experiences of Black girls are enough to offer new insights into theology.

Throughout this book, I have reflected on my own experiences during Black girlhood that shaped my theological framework. These experiences began with my dedication as a baby at Bethany Baptist Church in the early 1980s. As my dad held me in his arms with my mother by his side and my godparents adjacent, my parents committed to raising me in accordance with the faith that had been passed down to them. Without being aware of it, this was my introduction to faith and religious community. The village of loved ones who surrounded me continued in that commitment. Mama Hattie and Aunt Mary were determined to demonstrate what it meant to "live like Jesus" before me, my siblings, and my cousins. Pastor Soaries and my childhood church home, First Baptist, nurtured me in my faith while instilling in me a social consciousness and preparing me to serve my community.

When I was baptized as a ten-year-old girl, I was mostly nervous about my hair getting wet or whether I would be able to hold my breath long enough when I was under the water. I had no idea what kind of spiritual journey lay ahead for me. I'm not sure what I envisioned, and I certainly did not consider how my experiences as a Black girl would shape who I am today. This was a subject I engaged in with some of my students. I wondered if they had thought past where they were now and if they ever imagined what their spiritual journeys would look like as adults.

"So, you're all in your teenage years. Ten years from now, if you could be anywhere in your faith, what would it look like?" I asked. "Are you hopeful that faith and spirituality will still be a part of your life when you're an adult?"

The girls took a long pause to think about it, as though they'd never considered the thought before, much like I hadn't at their age. Their responses were thoughtful and honest.

For me, ten years from now I'm hoping that my faith will increase a lot and that I won't have any doubts or anything. Or like questioning. I'm hoping that I'll be able to focus on my spiritual walk and look back and say that I did everything that I had to do and that I'm not questioning God as much as I probably am now as a thirteen-year-old. I'm sure I'll still have questions, but I'm hoping as I get older those questions will start to go away.—Jewel, 13

It's kind of weird . . . I've been in church so long, I think I'll want to get out because I've heard everything. I don't know if

I'll be going to church. Or maybe not as much as my parents go every Sunday, but I'll probably just hop in every once in a while to get that feeling.—Tahirah, 16

Truthfully, I do want to find faith. I do. I want to be saved, but I don't know what I'm looking for and how to get to it.—London, 16

Because church has been a part of my upbringing, it's a part of me. So it has that semblance of home. It's what I grew up with. Even though I'm not very strong in my faith, it's something I will want to fall back on still.—Harmony, 17

My desire for myself is to find a balance of not having two polar worlds. I hope that one day my faith and my personal life would merge. I hope my faith is more present in my life, not just when I'm at church. I have such a grounded spiritual home, but how will that look when I'm at college? When I don't have my mom praying right there every time I come to share with her something that's going on. I wonder about that. I'm not sure what it will look like, but I hope that I can still have it in my life.—Camryn, 18

Regardless of the nuance of their responses, within them I see a consistent thread of hope. The girls are hopeful that their questions will lead to answers. They are hopeful that their future selves will grow and not abandon the faith that has been instilled in them as girls. They may not know where the spiritual journey will lead, but they are hopeful that they will get there.

NOTES

Introduction

1. Toni Morrison, "Toni Morrison on Love and Writing (Part One)," interview with Bill Moyers, March 11, 1990, https://billmoyers.com/content/toni-morrison-part-1.

2. N. Lynne Westfield, *Dear Sisters: A Womanist Practice of Hospitality* (Cleveland: Pilgrim Press, 2001), 8.

3. Stephanie Y. Mitchem, *Introducing Womanist Theology* (Maryknoll, NY: Orbis Books, 2002), 39.

4. Corinne T. Field and LaKisha Michelle Simmons, eds., *The Global History of Black Girlhood* (Urbana: University of Illinois Press, 2022), 4.

5. "Journey to Liberation: The Legacy of Womanist Theology," YouTube, educational video, 1:30, https://www.youtube.com/watch?v=PjhtUGqFCWg&t=330s.

6. Alice Walker, *In Search of Our Mothers' Gardens* (San Diego: Harcourt Brace Jovanovich, 1983), xi.

7. "What Manner of Woman: A Short Documentary Film," YouTube, educational video, 3:58, https://www.youtube.com/watch?v=sUlc6L1Z9-k.

8. "What Manner of Woman," 4:37.

9. Field and Simmons, *Global History of Black Girlhood*, 40.

10. Jemar Tisby (@JemarTisby), "Just because a white, Western male is doing theology doesn't necessarily mean it's wrong or bad,

but the picture is incomplete." X (formerly Twitter), March 14, 2022, 9:24, https://twitter.com/JemarTisby/status/1503361494435741700.

Chapter 1 Woman*ish* Theology of Scripture

1. Merijohn Wilken and Kristoffer Kristofferson, "One Day at a Time" (Nashville: Buckhorn Music Publishing Co., 1974).

2. Mitzi J. Smith, "Womanist Biblical Hermeneutics," YouTube, book promotion video, 1:22, https://www.youtube.com/watch?v=8PiRLmKDZEI.

3. Stephanie Y. Mitchem, *Introducing Womanist Theology* (Maryknoll, NY: Orbis Books, 2002), 117.

4. Walter B. Shurden, *The Baptist Identity: Four Fragile Freedoms* (Macon, GA: Smyth & Helwys, 2013), 13.

5. Deborah De Sousa Owens, "The Bible's Influence: The Bible in Black America," *New York Times*, December 11, 2014, https://www.washingtontimes.com/news/2014/dec/11/the-bibles-influence-the-bible-in-black-america/.

6. Marnita Coleman, "Telling Our Story: A Look at the History Passed Down via Church and the Family Bible," *AFRO News*, June 18, 2023, https://afro.com/telling-our-story-a-look-at-the-history-passed-down-via-church-and-the-family-bible/.

7. Katie Geneva Cannon, *Katie's Canon: Womanism and the Soul of the Black Community*, expanded 25th anniversary ed. (Minneapolis: Fortress, 2021), 56.

8. Kelly Brown Douglas, "Marginalized People, Liberating Perspectives," in *I Found God in Me: A Womanist Biblical Hermeneutics Reader*, ed. Mitzi J. Smith (Eugene, OR: Cascade Books, 2015), 82.

Chapter 2 Woman*ish* Theology of Salvation

1. Full lyrics for the spiritual song "Take Me to the Water" are available at https://hymnary.org/text/take_me_to_the_water.

2. Daniel Migliore, *Faith Seeking Understanding: An Introduction to Christian Theology* (Grand Rapids: Eerdmans, 2004), 423.

3. "And he said to them, 'Go into all the world and proclaim the good news to the whole creation. The one who believes and is baptized will be saved, but the one who does not believe will be condemned'" (Mark 16:15–16).

4. DC '94 was hosted by the organization Youth for Christ, whose mission was teenage evangelism.

5. In the 1990s, the Christian church was saturated with warnings around salvation and sex—otherwise known as "purity culture." Purity culture promoted a binary view of sexuality that relied on fear-based messaging using language that instilled anxiety, shame, or fear of consequences into our young minds. While the goal was to promote morally based standards of behavior, the result was that sex was presented as sinful and put our salvation at risk. This (incorrect) linking of salvation with ethical conduct was a source of confusion for me and many others.

6. Migliore, *Faith Seeking Understanding*, 423.

7. Migliore, *Faith Seeking Understanding*, 423.

Chapter 3 Woman*ish* Theology of the *Imago Dei*

1. Langston Hughes, "I, Too," in *The Collected Works of Langston Hughes* (2002), Poetry Foundation, https://www.poetryfoundation.org/poems/47558/i-too.

2. Khristi Lauren Adams, *Parable of the Brown Girl: The Sacred Lives of Girls of Color* (Minneapolis: Fortress, 2020), 26.

3. Nastassja E. Swift, "Conscious of Being Seen," in *The Global History of Black Girlhood*, ed. Corinne T. Field and LaKisha Michelle Simmons (Urbana: University of Illinois Press, 2022), 111.

4. Keturah Clark Colgate, "Black Hair and the *Imago Dei*: An Embodiment for God's Vision of Wholeness" (master's thesis, Rochester Crozer Divinity School, 2018), 1.

5. Adams, *Parable of the Brown Girl*, 36–37.

6. Kevin M. Young (@kevinmyoung), "Imagine how America would be different if every generation had grown up with only brown-eyed, dark-skinned images of Jesus and the disciples. Imagine how diversity would be embraced in America if the explorers and founders had never seen a blue-eyed, white-skinned image of Christ," X (formerly Twitter), August 27, 2023, 8:35 a.m., https://twitter.com/kevinmyoung/status/1695777056607363320.

7. Christena Cleveland, "God Is a Black Woman (Episode 8)," *Breaking Down Patriarchy* (podcast), February 21, 2023, https://breakingdownpatriarchy.com/episode-8-god-is-a-black-woman-with-dr-christena-cleveland/.

8. Yolanda Pierce, *In My Grandmother's House: Black Women, Faith, and the Stories We Inherit* (Minneapolis: Broadleaf Books, 2021), 2.

9. Pierce, *In My Grandmother's House*, 3.

10. Adams, *Parable of the Brown Girl*, 39.

11. Ebony M. Smith, "Society Thinks Black Girls Are Ugly," *Harvard Crimson*, February 10, 2022, https://www.thecrimson.com/article/2022/2/10/smith-bhm-oped/.

Chapter 4 Woman*ish* Theodicy

1. Associated Press, "Police Say Man Killed Wife, Girl, and Himself," *New York Times*, May 26, 1998, https://www.nytimes.com/1998/05/26/nyregion/metro-news-briefs-new-jersey-police-say-man-killed-wife-girl-and-himself.html.

2. Daniel Migliore, *Faith Seeking Understanding: An Introduction to Christian Theology* (Grand Rapids: Eerdmans, 2004), 426.

3. Xscape, "The Arms of the One Who Loves You," written by Diane Eve Warren, from the album *Traces of My Lipstick* (Atlanta: So So Def/Sony, 1998).

4. Fred Hammond and Radical for Christ, "No Way, No Way (You Won't Lose)," written by Fred Hammond and Kim Rutherford, from the album *Pages of Life* (Carlsbad, CA: Verity Records, 1998).

5. Theodorus P. van Baaren and Matt Stefon, s.v. "providence," *Britannica*, accessed December 8, 2023, https://www.britannica.com/topic/Providence-theology.

6. Migliore, *Faith Seeking Understanding*, 129.

7. "Trouble Don't Last Always" is the title of a popular song by Rev. Timothy Wright.

8. Jamie T. Phelps, "Joy Came in the Morning Risking Death and Resurrection: Confronting the Evil of Social Sin and Socially Sinful Structures," in *A Troubling in My Soul: Womanist Perspectives on Evil and Suffering*, ed. Emilie M. Townes (Maryknoll, NY: Orbis Books, 1993), 48.

9. Shawn Arango Ricks, "Falling through the Cracks: Black Girls and Education," *Interdisciplinary Journal of Teaching and Learning* 4, no. 2 (Spring 2014): 16, https://files.eric.ed.gov/fulltext/EJ1063223.pdf.

10. This is also known as process philosophy or ontology.

Chapter 5 Woman*ish* Theology of Prayer

1. Yolanda Pierce, *In My Grandmother's House: Black Women, Faith, and the Stories We Inherit* (Minneapolis: Broadleaf Books, 2021), 4.

2. Pierce, *In My Grandmother's House*, 4.

3. Pierce, *In My Grandmother's House*, 5.
4. Pierce, *In My Grandmother's House*, 13–14.
5. Melva Wilson Costen, "The Prayer Tradition of Black Americans," *Reformed Liturgy and Music* 15, no 2 (Spring 1981): 2, 86.
6. Dr. Anita Phillips, "The African American Tradition of Prayer," YouTube video, March 12, 2015, 7:20, https://www.youtube.com/watch?v=YqaOS6t3H4g&t=920s.
7. Helen Baylor, "Helen Baylor's Testimony: Praying Grandmother," YouTube video, August 1, 2015, 4:05, https://www.youtube.com/watch?v=Cus0WratJU8.
8. Kacie Starr Triplett, "Black Family: Let's Pray Together," Thy BlackMan.com, September 24, 2011, https://thyblackman.com/2011/09/24/black-family-lets-pray-together/.
9. Natalie Humphrey, Honore Hughes, and Deserie Holmes, "Understanding of Prayer among African American Children: Preliminary Themes," *Journal of Black Psychology* 34, no. 3 (2008): 309–30.
10. Humphrey, Hughes, and Holmes, "Understanding of Prayer," 312.
11. Humphrey, Hughes, and Holmes, "Understanding of Prayer," 320.
12. Humphrey, Hughes, and Holmes, "Understanding of Prayer," 320.

Chapter 6 Woman*ish* Theology of Hospitality

1. N. Lynne Westfield, *Dear Sisters: A Womanist Practice of Hospitality* (Cleveland: Pilgrim Press, 2001), vii.
2. Mary W. Anderson, "Hospitality Theology," *Christian Century* (July 1998): 643, https://www.religion-online.org/article/hospitality-theology-gen-181-10a-col-115-28-lk-1038-42.
3. Westfield, *Dear Sisters*, 26.
4. Westfield, *Dear Sisters*, 49.
5. Westfield, *Dear Sisters*, 41.
6. Henri J. M. Nouwen, *Reaching Out* (New York: Doubleday, 1975), 65–66.
7. Nouwen, *Reaching Out*, 66.
8. Westfield, *Dear Sisters*, 48.
9. Westfield, *Dear Sisters*, 64.
10. Khristi Lauren Adams, *Parable of the Brown Girl: The Sacred Lives of Girls of Color* (Minneapolis: Fortress, 2020), 50–51.

Chapter 7 Woman*ish* Theology of Service

1. Khristi Lauren Adams, *Unbossed: How Black Girls Are Leading the Way* (Minneapolis: Broadleaf Books, 2022), 65.

2. Melissa V. Harris-Perry, *Sister Citizen: Shame, Stereotypes, and Black Women in America* (New Haven: Yale University Press, 2011), 235.

3. Adams, *Unbossed*, 75.

Conclusion

1. Khristi Lauren Adams, *Parable of the Brown Girl: The Sacred Lives of Girls of Color* (Minneapolis: Fortress, 2020), 136–37.

KHRISTI LAUREN ADAMS (MDiv, Princeton Theological Seminary) is a speaker, writer, youth advocate, and ordained Baptist minister. She is the award-winning author of *Parable of the Brown Girl* (named the Best Young Adult Book by the African American Literary Awards and the New York Black Librarians Caucus) as well as *Unbossed: How Black Girls Are Leading the Way* and its middle-grade version, *Black Girls Unbossed: Young World Changers Leading the Way*. Adams formerly worked as dean of spiritual life and equity at The Hill School in Pottstown, Pennsylvania, and now is the executive director of community and belonging at The St. Paul's Schools in Maryland.

CONNECT WITH KHRISTI:

KhristiLaurenAdams.com

Khristi Lauren Adams, Author

@KhristiLauren

@KhristiAdams